Help in the Classroom

Second Edition

Maggie Balshaw

David Fulton Publishers
London

David Fulton Publishers Ltd
414 Chiswick High Road, London W4 5TF
www.fultonpublishers.co.uk

First published in Great Britain by David Fulton Publishers 1999
Reprinted 2000, 2001, 2003 (twice)
10 9 8 7 6 5

British Library Cataloguing in Publication Data
A catalogue record for this book is available from the British Library.

ISBN 1-85346-476-7

Typeset by FSH Print & Production Ltd, London
Printed and bound in Great Britain

Contents

Acknowledgements

This book, like the earlier one, would not have been written without the help and support of my 'critical friend'. As I recounted previously, he said in 1991 that you learn much more by writing a book than from reading one. I still agree with him about that!

One of the chief reasons for that agreement is how much I have learnt through the ongoing research I have carried out between that edition in 1991 and this one. I could not have written what is to be found in this updated version if colleagues in many schools, colleges and LEAs, both here in the UK and in other countries, had not given me valuable time and, more importantly, crucial insights into their work. Of course, in particular I must single out countless learning support assistants who have told me so openly, graphically and succinctly about the world of their practice. The power of this book, I feel, is that it is rooted in and written from that practice. In particular, I feel that the book's strength lies in examining situations where reflective assistants and teachers have been reviewing and developing their work in partnership together. The book analyses and portrays that practice, rather than being written from other professionals' points of view, which are not always a reflection of the reality of the busy, crowded everyday lives and practice at 'the cutting edge' which is the classroom.

Since the writing of the original version of this book, other authors and professionals, including the new occupants of the Department for Education and Employment, have added their valuable and positive contributions to this increasingly important aspect of educational practice. This has widened the debate and discourse about the most effective ways of managing, supporting and training learning support assistants in their valuable and indispensable contribution to the work of schools. These schools are seeking to offer the best possible learning opportunities for their children and students, whatever the diversity of their learning needs.

Therefore, with much gratitude I dedicate this edition of the book to learning support assistants everywhere, and hope that the words and ideas within it support them and their schools in their quest to develop equitable and effective practice which takes account of the learning needs of all children and students.

Maggie Balshaw
Cambridge
May 1999

Author's Note

In re-writing *Help in the Classroom*, I spent some time considering whether the title does justice to the contents. When writing the book originally during 1989–90, I felt that the title *did* then reflect the ways in which the work of the Learning Support Assistant (LSA) was seen by many professionals in schools and LEAs.

Now though, I think that the title is perhaps out-dated. The role of the LSA has moved forward considerably in terms of its development and in the ways that people expect it to be seen, both now and in the future. Rather than merely being seen as a 'helper' in the classroom, today's LSAs, where practice is effective, are seen as 'partners' in the classroom. However, on balance it seemed wise to stick with the original title. As the book has become well known in professional circles, changing its name might only serve to confuse busy people.

I hope therefore that LSAs will forgive me for, in the title only, portraying them as 'helpers', which they indeed are, but then they are so much more, as I'm sure those who either read further or are intimately concerned with the job already know!

Introduction

The aim of this book is to help schools to make better use of the resources of learning support assistants. It begins by examining the work of assistants who are employed to support the learning of children seen as having special educational needs. It outlines the major issues that I have found to be important with regard to the assistants' management, support and training. A key feature of this is the need for much of their staff development opportunities to be sited in school in order for training to be relevant, i.e. to meet the contextual needs of the assistants as they work as part of the overall provision to support the learning of a wide range of children and students.

Chapter 3 explains why this school-sited staff development is most likely to be effective if it is seen as an aspect of school development. It endorses the notion of supporting change in schools through processes of staff development. The key proposal is that, in order to take account of the ways in which adults learn best about their practice, 'collaborative inquiry' should be the strategy used. Collaborative inquiry involves all adults exploring their working practice together on an equal footing, and agreeing goals for development.

It is recommended that this inquiry might take place at two levels. First, there is the examination and development of practice in the classroom within existing school policies and guidelines. Second, there is a more fundamental consideration and review of how both classroom and school practice and policy might develop. This review is based on a series of principles developed as a result of research into assistants' working lives. The resources offered in Part Two are practical guidelines on how to develop the inquiry process. There is a set of core activities and also an extension set, focused on primary practice, secondary practice and also assistants' learning and practice, with guidance given about the size and type of inquiry groups with which they might be used.

The book offers what might still be seen as a radical stance with regard to assistants working in the field of special educational needs in that it does not provide the more traditional range of tips and skills for staff working with children and students seen as having educational difficulties of various types or categories. Rather, in order to get away from potential labels for both pupils and assistants, it considers learning opportunities instead of learning deficits.

Part One offers the background and rationale for the practical activities which form the second part. The readership for Part One is anyone who is interested in the reasoning behind the activities. It is essential reading for members of school staff who may choose to coordinate some work in the school based on the materials in Part Two. Of particular importance is Chapter 4, which offers comprehensive instructions and support to the coordinator of 'collaborative inquiry' in a school.

Part 1

CONTEXT AND RATIONALE

1 Examining the work of learning support assistants

This chapter explains the reasons that led to the original writing of this book. It tells what prompted my interest and inquiry into the working lives of assistants. There is an explanation of how learning support assistants have become such a significant part of the provision in schools over the last fifteen years or so. There follows a brief description of the research inquiries I have carried out, both initially and subsequently, drawing out the significant issues as I see them with regard to the social aspects of assistants' working contexts and conditions. The analogy is drawn between the continuing tensions and struggles at a basic conceptual level that the whole educational system is experiencing, and the kinds of tensions experienced by the assistants with whom I have worked. An explanation of what might be done about this, and a suggestion about the actions that schools might take to resolve the difficulties I have found, are also offered. Of particular significance is the issue of where and how assistants are best trained in order to meet their professional needs and the needs of the schools in which they work.

What created the initial interest and inquiry?

I first became particularly interested in the work of assistants as long ago as 1986, although prior to that I had experienced as a class teacher the invaluable support they could provide, in both special and mainstream settings. The more specific interest began when I was newly appointed to a post in an LEA as coordinator for special educational needs. Among my accountabilities was that of jointly planning, coordinating and presenting in-service training (INSET) opportunities for what were then known as special needs assistants. I also met assistants in their own school contexts when I was there in a professional direction and support capacity with both teachers and assistants.

Meeting assistants in both their school situations and during their INSET courses made me realise the complexity of situations in which they find themselves. The wide-ranging nature of their work, the ways in which they are expected to function, and the complex nature of their management and support became apparent to me. As coordinator for special educational needs I also had a brief to monitor both the success and effectiveness of the INSET courses, and the management and support offered to assistants in schools.

I was particularly struck by the avid way in which those assistants fortunate enough to secure places on the INSET courses lapped up the

---

opportunity to learn, develop confidence and skills and, perhaps more importantly, chew over their situations and problems with each other. The floodgates opened when they compared notes with each other about their relative experiences in schools. This happened when they did it formally, with a particular focus during course sessions, and informally, in conversation over coffee. It gave assistants the opportunity to offer each other and me some very explicit observations. These were about their roles, people's attitudes towards them and their feelings about all this. Here are just three examples, which provide the reader with a flavour of some of the issues raised about ten years ago.

> I wanted to go to a meeting after school when AB (an officer of the LEA) was to talk about special needs and everything, and I was told it was nothing to do with me, it was for teachers.

(A particularly ironical situation, since the officer mentioned held the budget that funded the assistant's allocation to the school.)

> I was talking to a parent the other day and she said 'Oh, you're the general dogsbody!'. I had to explain what I did, I was very upset about this.

(One wonders why the parent didn't know the reasons for the assistant's presence.)

> The other thing is, when you have lessons and they've got cover like I had on Friday last week. We had a French lesson, the member of staff taking over had no idea about French, the children had got work to do, so you know, who goes round to help them? I do! And you know, I don't mind, but I think, 'Well, the teaching staff are getting five times the amount of money I'm getting!'

(She definitely has a point!)

I was so struck by these situations and comments, that it seemed at the time to be crucial that all these experiences and feelings should be harnessed in a form that might help to analyse them and recommend some form of action. This led me to carry out an inquiry into the working lives of assistants. In more recent times I have reinvestigated their work, and have continued to ask questions about the practice surrounding them. Subsequently, when I have asked assistants in the last year what are the most stressful aspects of their jobs, some examples from many they have offered have been:

- not knowing teachers' expectations
- being put in at the deep end
- staff and student relationships
- trying to please
- temporary contracts.

It seems to me that many of the experiences I examined in order to write the first version of this book are still occuring in schools up and down the UK, albeit in the context of further government reforms. Hence the need for an updated version! So this book is a culmination of the outcomes of both my original inquiries and more recent ones.

What led to the increase of assistants in schools?

In England and Wales the original catalyst for this was the Warnock report (DES 1978). In the twenty years since then there have been many other influences, starting with the 1981 Education Act. LEAs were charged through this legislation with increasing their range of provision for children seen as having special educational needs.

National developments subsequently have been influenced by moves towards more integration into mainstream schools of those children seen as having difficulties of a wide variety, thus putting pressure on schools to develop approaches that cater for a wider range of diversity. Pressure groups, which include parents and disability advocates, have been influential in moving schools towards a more open-door policy. International developments also have encouraged the notion of inclusion at a more global level, through the platform in particular of human rights issues and such edicts as Education for All (Unesco 1990) and the Salamanca Statement (Unesco 1994). All of this has encouraged a shift from integration to inclusion, where the emphasis has been moved from the modification of approaches towards individuals to the rethinking of the nature of school systems and their work in accommodating all children. This argument is based on the notion that special needs should be seen as a school development task, where schools see the challenge as one of developing their approaches, both curricular and organisational, in order to cater for as wide a range of diversity as possible, rather than focusing on attempting to compensate for the deficits of individuals.

At the same time and parallel to these worldwide developments, in this country there has been a seemingly directly contrary development nationally, where schools have been judged by their assessment and examination results, and put into competing positions with one another. Therefore, schools have been faced with the dilemma of raising standards in a competitive environment, while fulfilling their moral obligations to a wider range of children, some of whom are seen by many as having the potential to lower the standards and averages of the school overall.

Consequently, a feature which emerged, as a trickle in the 1980s but rapidly increasing later, particularly since schools have handled devolved or grant maintained budgets, was the appointment of assistants as part of the provision for special needs. As a result, LEAs began to employ gradually larger and larger numbers of assistants, mainly unqualified, to work in schools. Taking this lead many more schools have followed suit, and chosen to appoint assistants to their staff, in many cases instead of teachers as a cost-saving ploy. There are, of course, moral and professional implications in these decisions, particularly where the most vulnerable children in the system are seen to be entrusted to those members of staff who on the face of it are the least qualified to work with them.

Recent surveys carried out in England have shown there to be the equivalent of 24,000 full-time assistants in primary schools alone. These and indeed other assistants' contributions are, in the words of the Green Paper of

---

1997, 'central to successful SEN practice in mainstream and special schools'. An increased interest from researchers is reflected in a growing number of surveys, research, and written pieces of evidence and advice. Sebba and Sachdev (1997) state that, in research observing effective practice with assistants which focuses on inclusion, certain factors should be present. Among these are the statement that 'the quality of joint planning is critical to the effective use of support in the classroom' and that 'support needs to be used flexibly to ensure that it enhances rather than impedes the process of inclusive education'.

Since my writing of the original version of this book, others have also been producing advice and support to schools about the ways in which assistants might work in order to meet the needs of children. Among these are Fox (1993, 1998) and Lorenz (1998), each of whom have focused in very practical ways on supporting assistants in their work. It is encouraging that in an area in which there was not a great deal of substantive writing when I first put my thoughts into book form a growing number of professionals are now offering helpful advice.

What's in a name?

There has been a recognition in recent times of the myriad of terms used to describe assistants and that this has served to cause some confusion. In the Green Paper of 1997 the Department for Education and Employment stated that a generic term might be advisable and suggested 'learning support assistant'. This seems a positive suggestion, since it does not label either child or assistant as 'special needs', potentially a stigma, and instead focuses on learning, which reflects a universal and inclusive aim for their work. There are still, however, many assistants who are known by other formal descriptions. Some examples are: special support assistant, key worker, ancillary, welfare assistant, special needs assistant, non-teaching assistant, teaching assistant, teacher aide and educational support worker.

I have also found many terms used to describe assistants that do not appear on a formal contract or job description. Some have been used directly, others have implied that this is how assistants are seen by others in the school community, or are how assistants feel they are seen by inference or treatment. Some positive examples are: interpreter, miracle worker, someone with worthwhile opinions, a valued member of the team. Less positive are: dumbo, jack of all trades, dogsbody, bouncer, personal servant.

What do assistants actually do?

Recently collected data about what assistants actually do leads me to reiterate an early set of ideas about the categories into which their tasks fall. In each of the categories originally drawn up as assistants carried out a role analysis during INSET activities, and which I documented in the first edition of this book, I continue to find examples such as the ones below.

Child/student contact activities:

curriculum and learning related

- using differentiated worksheets
- coordinating small group activities
- using particular skills to contribute to class lessons

pastoral care related

- being a 'listening ear'
- sorting out disputes over equipment, space or activities
- maintaining continuity of behaviour management policies

aspects of physical support

- toileting
- lifting
- maintaining hearing aids, braillers, keyboards and wheelchairs during lessons.

Non-contact activities:

ancillary/preparation tasks

- cataloguing reading books
- producing worksheets on word processors
- recording television programmes

liaison and coordination tasks

- producing written reports for reviews
- writing to parents in home–school communication books
- passing on information orally between members of staff.

I have subsequently also asked assistants in a wide range of working contexts to describe the most rewarding aspects of their role and these are some examples:

- child's independence
- positive relationships
- praise and appreciation
- opinions sought
- classed as a team member.

Taking the role analysis a step forward I have also asked about the challenging aspects experienced by assistants, and here are some examples:

- how much input, initiative to use
- involving child fully in class situations
- 'on the spot' situations
- gaining credibility with staff and children
- just doing the job.

Many of these challenges and others like them present an opportunity to consider the issue of staff development.

What are the staff development needs of assistants?

The kinds of challenges documented above offer clues to staff development needs. Many of these challenges are evidence of the kinds of support for assistants' work that are required, such as the need for more curriculum-based knowledge and skills; interpersonal skills; assertiveness skills; responding professionally to awkward situations. In evaluating in-service courses offered to assistants outside schools it may be found that some of these needs might indeed be met. However, my research has shown that positive outcomes identified by assistants, such as increased confidence and skills, meeting other assistants, and identifying further training needs were counterbalanced by what I have termed the 'three Rs'. These are relevance, relationships and resentment. 'Relevance' refers to the limitations that externally held courses have to the context in which the assistant works, resulting in only partial relevance of course contents to actual working practice. 'Relationships' refers to the inability of external courses to deal with the complex relationships that exist in any school context in any meaningful way. 'Resentment' refers to the fact that assistants often learn new skills and practices on courses which they are not always given the opportunity to use back in school. Having said this I am not suggesting that external courses are irrelevant, but that they should offer opportunities for accreditation and formal recognition, along with attempting to optimally relate their contents to the competencies and skills needed in the particular contexts in which assistants work.

This evaluation brought me to a realisation that in order for some of the assistants' staff development needs to be met ideally much of their training should take place in situ, in the school, and that therefore schools should be encouraged to recognise this and provide context and practice related opportunities for assistants.

Of course, some of the challenges presented in the data lead to the identification of staff development needs beyond assistants themselves. I stated in the first edition of this book that there was a need for teachers to learn how to manage the assistants' time, and organise the classroom to take account of more than one adult working with the children. I am pleased to see that in more recent times there has been recognition in the Department for Education and Employment that this is a priority area for development, and that in England the Teacher Training Agency is recommending the need to create opportunities for teacher learning at both initial teacher training level and during in-service training. This follows my advice and that of Sebba and Sachdev (1997), who suggest that 'traditionally, teachers have not been trained to work with other adults in the classroom. Initial teacher education and continuing professional development will need to address this.'

Changes in recent years in the structure of special needs provision have led to the central role of what are known in the UK as special needs coordinators

(SENCOs). This term, along with many others which are in current use, supports the maintenance of the status quo in special needs terminology. As coordinators they are seen as central to the management of learning support assistants, therefore the staff development needs of both the assistants and their teaching colleagues form an important aspect of their roles. Perhaps if they were also called learning support coordinators there would seem to be more commonality with the assistants in their task. The traditional special needs label would also be taken away, in accordance with seeking to develop more inclusive practice. This leads me to explore the tensions that schools experience, given the pressure I mentioned with regard to current developments worldwide and closer to home over special needs.

What are the tensions associated with the role of assistants in schools?

The ethos and culture of schools, which are themselves attempting to come to terms with the tensions associated with special needs issues, impact upon the work of assistants. A tension felt by assistants is that of the attitudes and expectations of teaching staff with respect to children seen as having special needs and their roles. One particular example is an emphasis on individual education plans rather than an inclusive orientation which encourages a flexibility of approach in classroom and school practices. If nothing else reveals tensions around assistants' roles, this does. They are often caught between, on the one hand, being seen as key users of individual plans and, on the other, the potential isolation to which that can lead, if mismanaged, for the assistants and the children. This becomes a form of 'in-class segregation', apart from the curriculum all other children are offered and are away from collaborative learning experiences with their peers. On the other hand, flexibly managed, their role minimises this segregation and leads to independent learning and support for a wide variety of children in the class. The flaw is that, because of bureaucratic procedures, the majority of assistants are allocated to an individual child and school staff and parents may see this as a 'right' which should not be diluted; also, for some teachers, it may provide a way of avoiding the responsibility of teaching children they see as difficult and for whom they lack confidence in planning their curricular approaches. They might also see it as a way of compensating for deficits, rather than an opportunity for learning.

What are the wider causes of the tensions that assistants experience? There are some fundamental underlying causes of tension which have an impact on assistants' work. I have already alluded to them earlier in the chapter in respect to the reasons for an increased number of assistants in schools. First, here is the tension between historical, and some would say outdated and traditional, views of special needs. The way in which developed education systems, such as those in the UK, the USA and some other European countries, have responded to these views is fundamentally different from the ideas and attitudes which currently abound worldwide about the nature of special needs and the aspirations of Education for All.

The examples above about attitudes to assistants and children are evidence of a legacy of these tensions. Where children are described as having difficulties and disabilities, singled out and labelled by teaching staff and others such as parents, governors and other children and students, then clearly the assistants working specifically with them are part of that segregated and individualising culture. Even the term SENCO is a feature of this perception, so that not only children are labelled. If the staff and others see the task in a wider, more flexible and creative way, then assistants are more likely to be seen as enhancing learning opportunities for all. However, in many schools there are tensions at policy and practice levels, often originating in individual perceptions and attitudes which can create the potential for confusion about what the assistants in the school should actually be doing.

Second, more specifically, there is the issue of how historical influences have left a legacy which is resource driven, these resources regarded as compensating for children seen as having disabilities or deficits in learning. The allocation of assistants on a one-to-one basis reflects this. Individual learning plans often focus on the individuals rather than on inclusive classroom processes and strategies, effective teaching and optimal learning opportunities for all children.

Many of these underlying tensions have been documented by others, such as Ainscow (1998), in more detail than I can do here, and I come back to the tensions created when changes are initiated as schools attempt to move from one position to another. Deep-rooted assumptions, understandings and attitudes, coupled with a reliance on previous and current practice, which often feels organisationally comfortable, are two of the major ones. Resourcing issues, which are a major influence in the UK and other developed countries, as I have outlined, on policy, provision and practice, particularly in LEAs, but also in schools, often depend on the bureaucratic framework of the assessment procedures and are seen as a series of hurdles to get over, with a pot of gold at the other side.

What do these potential tensions mean for your school?

As you read of these tensions you will perhaps feel that you too are in the middle of a struggle, that this resonates to a greater or lesser extent with the culture of your own school. All schools are likely to be involved in this struggle. However, some school staff perhaps do not realise the impact it can have on the work of assistants.

I hope that you, in reading this, are able to relate to the issues I have outlined, and how it affects your own context. Where schools in other countries are struggling with a dearth of resources of the kind that tend to be taken for granted here in the UK they are seeing the necessity to look for resources that are 'free'. These include human resources. This involves creativity and capacity building, where both adults and children are seen as the two great resources for learning, which should be appreciated and built on. This means working collaboratively together, learning how to respond to diversity, adult to adult, adult to child(ren), child to child. In some ways the people in these countries are lucky, they have no history of established special needs bureaucracy to change, only opportunities to see. Despite the fact that children carry their chairs to school, or are sent home when the monsoon comes through the leaky roof or have only one textbook between sixty or more children, they see the ordinary classroom as the place where 'education for all' takes place.

Here, and in other sophisticated education systems around the world, the task is to see a way through the tensions and struggles I have outlined. In the next chapter I go on to explore the key areas which I feel need to be addressed with respect to these issues and others. In schools where assistants feel a much greater sense of job satisfaction and self esteem certain conditions have been found to exist. What are these?

2 Developing policy and practice

This chapter outlines the rationale behind the six principles on which the activities in Part Two are based. It goes on to explain the necessity to decide on how to use the activities, whether at the level of reviewing practice with teaching staff and assistants who are working together in classrooms; or of a review of policy and practice at whole school level; or of the extension activities which encourage further development of ideas at either level.

Six principles

It is possible to consider practice in the school, while keeping in mind the notion of the 'struggles' I described in Chapter 1, and the school's place in these. It is possible then to move forward as the result of this review. Using the six principles offered here it is possible to review the school's practice and, if it is wished, its policy.

The activities in Part Two are presented in six sets, and for each there are extension activities. There are indicators which guide their use in pairs and small groups, larger groups, and whole school staff sessions. The activities are intended to be used in a practical manner to create the climate for a collaborative inquiry into the school's practice and policy. It is essential to read the rationale behind the principles before attempting to apply the activities in practice.

The headings in italics which follow the principles on the list are actual quotes from assistants about their perceived lot in life, and relate directly to the issues covered by that particular principle.

The six principles are:

- **Roles and responsibilities:** learning support assistants should be clear about their roles and responsibilities, and not be *piggies-in-the-middle*
- **Communication:** learning support assistants should be included in and understand the communication system in the school, not to be left in *no-man's-land*
- **Consistency of approach:** learning support assistants should be seen positively as part of the provision to meet children's and students' educational needs, not as *dogsbodies*
- **A working team:** learning support assistants should be valued members of a working team, not seen as the *spy in the classroom*
- **Personal and professional skills:** learning support assistants should be encouraged to make use of their personal and professional skills, not treated as an *overgrown pupil*

- **Staff development needs:** learning support assistants should be supported in the development of their professional skills, not *left up in the air*.

Roles and responsibilities

Learning support assistants should be clear about their roles and responsibilities. Assistants who feel as if they are *piggies-in-the-middle* are hardly going to feel that they are clear about what they should be doing. Quite the opposite, assistants should be involved in drawing up their roles and responsibilities, and in reviewing and updating them on a regular basis. All teaching colleagues should also be aware of these roles and responsibilities in order that expectations and accountabilities are clear and that their requests to assistants are appropriate and consistent with agreed job descriptions.

Communication

Learning support assistants should be included in and understand the communication system in the school. Assistants who feel they are in a kind of *no-man's-land* are unlikely to be sure about what they ought to be doing, without sufficient information and knowledge about the school system. Instead, assistants should be kept up to date with necessary and essential information with regard to children and students, such as plans for their learning, the lessons in which they are involved, the curriculum aims and objectives. In fact, they should be drawn into the planning processes of the school in appropriate ways.

Consistency of approach

Learning support assistants should be seen positively as part of the provision to meet children's and students' educational needs. Assistants who feel that they are *dogsbodies* are hardly likely to be positive about the ways in which they are seen, with their self-esteem potentially lowered by this state of affairs. Rather, a positive attitude to assistants should lead to a consistency of approach among adults in supporting inclusive practices and to development of confidence and self-esteem in assistants; professional regard for them then develops among the school community, including parents and governors; they become at ease in using their initiative, with the management and support of their teaching colleagues.

A working team

Learning support assistants should be part of a working team. Assistants who feel that they are treated like *spies in the classroom* are unlikely to feel welcome, while at the same time experiencing being put on the spot by other members of staff asking them to disclose information about the classroom situations and colleagues with whom they work. Instead they should feel valued members of the working team, which might be a small partnership team, a wider departmental team, the whole school team or the community team; the assistants should be valued for the contributions they make to any or all of those teams in ways that are made explicit to them, thus setting up an ethos and climate of respect among the adults that communicates itself to the children and students.

Personal and professional skills

Learning support assistants should be encouraged to make use of their personal and professional skills. Assistants who spend some of their time feeling like *overgrown pupils* are not going to feel encouraged to offer whatever skills, experience and knowledge they do possess, or feel encouraged to identify staff development needs. Rather assistants, in using their personal and professional skills to the full in broadening curriculum approaches, add strength and depth to the overall skills and expertise on offer; at the same time they should be supported with any identified professional weaknesses; and be offered appropriate opportunities for professional development.

Staff development needs

Learning support assistants should be supported in the development of their professional skills. Assistants who consider themselves *left up in the air*, having been promised training and staff development opportunities which fail to materialise, will not feel encouraged in the development of their professional skills, being more likely to experience frustration at knowing what they would like to learn, without getting the chance to learn it. Instead assistants should be supported in their professional development, which should take place wherever possible alongside teaching staff in classrooms and in staff development sessions with wider groups of school staff; this should be in school wherever appropriate, but also outside school, making use of courses available through the LEA or other organisations in order to pursue skill development and learning appropriate to the job. Wherever possible this should lead to qualifications, recognised locally and nationally and thus enhancing status, and, where individuals wish it, to career progression.

Commentary

In presenting these six principles there are two areas which need additional explanation. One is the interlinked nature of the issues addressed by the six principles and therefore of the activities outlined in Part Two. In some ways I have put in arbitrary divisions to streamline the process. The issues in all areas are so interwoven and interdependent that these arbitrary divisions appear to cut through the threads. It will be found that, as the activities are used, it will be necessary to consider some of the issues that seem to belong somewhere else. This is very understandable and quite acceptable, and it will in fact help with the realisation that the assistants' work is in itself a reflection of these complex interwoven policy issues. It is not easy to divide them into neat compartments. However, at a pragmatic level, in order to work with the issues systematically and give each due care and attention it should be helpful to have these divisions. Coordinators will feel that the activities are more under control, in both their use and their scope.

The second issue meriting further explanation is that of the scope and the level at which the activities might be used in the school. The question for consideration is: how far-reaching are these activities expected to be, with their implicit challenges to classroom practice and, more fundamentally, to the whole-school policy? Whoever is responsible for coordinating any development will have to take this decision, in collaboration with colleagues, using these ideas and activities with assistants and teachers in the school.

The activities can in fact be used at two levels:

1. involving a consideration of how practice might be developed within existing policy;
2. involving a consideration of how both practice and school policy might be developed.

The coordinator needs to be aware that starting the process at level 1 is quite likely to lead at some stage to level 2 activities. The question at this point therefore has to be: 'Can we handle this, as individuals, as a team, as a school?'

At level 1 the issue is about doing better whatever is already being done, within the existing policy, i.e. 'doing things right' in the area of classroom practice. Level 2, on the other hand, is about attempting to 'do the right thing' in the school as a whole, and in particular with respect to more recent attitudes and approaches to special educational needs. That is not to say the activities attempt to prescribe a policy for special needs in any individual school as a whole. It would be insensitive for an outsider, such as myself, to do so. The policy should be devised by the personnel within the school. The policy of the school could well reflect the newer means of conceptualising special needs in a way that fits the context of the school. If the school is ready to reconsider, or is already reconsidering, its view on the links between developing inclusive practices, in order to welcome and cater for a wide range of diversity, and school development, then the practice surrounding the work of assistants is a crucial part of that process of inclusion. Therefore, the activities in this book are supportive of those ambitions. They do not reflect a view that concentrates on assistants compensating for weaknesses in individual children, so that these children can fit into a largely unchanged system, where little fundamental change in attitude and practice happens.

However, I refer here back to my argument in Chapter 1. This is that if schools continue to see assistants as a reflection of the compensation for deficits in learning due to children's inherent difficulties or disabilities, then it is possible to improve that form of practice. The systems current in many developed countries, including the UK, tend to focus on the identification of difficulties, tie this closely to the subsequent allocation of resources, and thus create a culture of targeting resources to individuals; so it is necessary to work largely within these parameters. Using some or all of the activities in the book could well lead to an attempt to do that. I myself recognise the dilemma of struggles between existing procedural influences and older perceptions of the special needs task on one side, and more creative and open perceptions of the task on the other. Most schools are caught in a mixture of the practice of the traditional and the vision, or, as some may well see it, the rhetoric of the new, and this author cannot attempt to guess at where any individual school is with regard to these complex issues.

'Doing the right thing' is the decision that the coordinator of these proposed developments would have to make in collaboration with colleagues, including managers of the school. I leave that to the reader at this point. Reviewing the situation in school is one way of coming to that decision, and in the next chapter I put forward my rationale for carrying out that review effectively, involving all the relevant people, and deciding what actions to take as a result of it.

3 Supporting change through staff development

This chapter is based on a set of assumptions, which are outlined. It also focuses on the needs of adult learners. Meeting these needs is more likely to be successful at an in-school level, and an explanation of this is offered through the idea of collaborative inquiry. The necessity to link these individual needs to school development is outlined. This is followed by an explanation of how to carry out a process of review and development within school, so that the school becomes a 'learning organisation' (Senge 1990), and offers some of the theory behind what is effective practice in this field.

Some basic assumptions

I start from a set of basic assumptions, and then illustrate these in more detail by incorporating them into my recommendation to carry out collaborative inquiry into the school's practice. These assumptions are drawn from my own experiences over a number of years in attempting to provide effective staff development opportunities for a range of staff. They are also drawn from various sources in the extensive literature about staff development. The assumptions are as follows:

- the notion of staff development as a way of bringing about development and change;
- the inclusion of all the relevant people in the collaborative inquiry;
- the use of a form of collaborative inquiry to bring about a review of need and a plan of activities;
- the expectation of a contribution to the process from all members of staff no matter where they exist within the hierarchy;
- the principle that all individual contributions are valued as worthwhile to the whole, so that people are resources to one another;
- the development of a collegiality which celebrates individual ideas and contributions, while helping the team to move forward productively.

Educational change and development

The experience of bringing about educational change and development is well documented in the literature. Probably the most well known proponent of what effective processes of change in educational contexts look like is

Michael Fullan. He states that for change to happen at all effectively it is important to involve those who will be bringing about the change in the planning of it. This increases the chance of them understanding why the change is needed, and how it should be brought about. If people are to understand the need for and the processes of change, then they need to 'make sense of it as a personal process'.

Fullan also recommends that staff development is one of the ways in which the process of change can be supported. Reviewing practice, the identification of areas for development, and collaborative planning of how to go about it, are all components of staff development. He also refers to the notion of adults as learners, and states that adults (staff) who learn together and therefore develop at a professional level within a collaborative environment are in a better position to carry out some effective developments. They will fare better than those who are expected to learn because somebody else decides on the need for change, plans the change on their behalf, then tells them to do it, without always laying out realistic strategies or timescales (Fullan 1990, 1991). Moreover, he puts forward the idea that 'what is worth fighting for in your school' is best determined from within (Fullan and Hargreaves 1992; Fullan 1993). This leads to the development of what he calls a 'learning organisation', based on the work of Senge (1990). This is an organisation which learns how changes are best managed in its own context, as well as about specific initiatives for change and that all participants in the process of change have learning needs related to that change.

It is worth mentioning at this point that my previous recommendations about situating staff development within schools in order to improve the work of assistants is confirmed by Fullan and his colleagues in this field. The idea that the adults, teachers and assistants, should learn together in the context which actually creates their staff development needs is linked to and should grow from policies for overall staff development.

Two important elements deserve further consideration here. These are fundamental elements of the processes of change. One is the degree of both commitment and control that participants in a change feel they have. The other is the emotionality of the change process. The analysis through research into the process of change has shown that these are both important features (Ainscow *et al.* 1994a). Where changes are imposed from outside there is often little commitment and even less control over these by the school staff. Creating an agenda for change from within a context means that there is likely to be a more mutually agreed commitment to the developments envisaged from individuals involved in the initiative. Moreover, they are also much more likely to feel they have control over what they choose to do, and how, and what kind of timescale is feasible.

Think of your own context, and how committed you were to something imposed from outside, and the control you personally had over it. Then think again, this time of a development you and some of your colleagues decided on. What degree of commitment and control did you feel you had? Which experience was more satisfactory, and which made a difference to effective classroom or school practice? How did you feel about each experience?

This brings me to another very important element, which is how people feel about the process of change generally, and feel specifically in regard to a particular one. A variety of emotions is associated with changes in schools, ranging from strongly positive ones, for example, feeling enthusiastic, exhilarated, committed, supported, to extremely negative ones such as feeling cynical, isolated, angry, or destabilised. Any form of change can cause turbulence, and indeed deep-rooted change, as Fullan says, has to create disturbance and challenge in order to succeed. Merely scratching the surface, tinkering around the edges so as not to create too much challenge to existing thinking and practice, will not encourage fundamental developments. But turbulence is largely related to emotionality. Hargreaves (1998) describes how too little attention has been paid to this aspect of the change process with a culture of 'Oh, they'll just have to get on with it!' being prevalent in educational change and development initiatives. The trouble with that stance is that it ignores the very emotionality which is fundamental to people understanding the specific change in which they are involved.

My own research, carried out over a period of several years, into what supports the learning of adults in order to bring about developments in classroom and school practice has also helped to shape the assumptions I have made and the collaborative inquiry processes I am recommending (Balshaw 1991, 1996a, 1996b; Balshaw *et al.* 1997; Balshaw 1998). I have found that it is crucial to recognise the challenge that is needed in order for learning to take place – whether this challenge is to perceptions, attitudes and beliefs, or to existing classroom practice or school policy. But balancing this challenge with support for learners as they go through a potentially difficult and complex experience is equally important. We are all more likely to take risks with our learning and maybe our practice if there is someone there, metaphorically at least, to hold our hand. Often this is best done in a partnership arrangement, which can be a helpful element of collaborative inquiry.

My research has shown that there are two important features of learning in this way. These are support and challenge. Supportive elements are:

- listening to each other;
- sharing ideas and concerns;
- being reflective together;
- relating to each other's contexts.

Challenging aspects are:

- inquiring further into ideas or opinions expressed;
- exploring together strategies for problem solving;
- establishing courses of action and their review;
- being constructively critical;
- building accountability to one another into their activities.

So, keeping these ideas in mind, I recommend a form of staff development which creates conditions that will facilitate adult learning. This approach is known as 'collaborative', following the ideas of Reason (1988), who describes it as a 'holistic learning process'. This approach involves staff in a given context developing personally and professionally as part of a team which reviews its practice regularly in a collaborative learning process, and thus fosters these conditions. Using collaborative inquiry implies that all of those involved (and in the case of this book, that includes assistants) are learners together about their work. This means starting with perceptions, attitudes and philosophy, and going on to address reviewing and planning, strategies and action, and using in-built procedures for monitoring and evaluating what they are doing together. As Reason states:

> the differences between inquiry, learning and action in the world become indistinct and unimportant, as we consider collaborative inquiry as a holistic learning process.

The emphasis on collaboration as a means of supporting change is promoted by Thousand and Villa (1991) who have been involved in work in schools in the USA which supports them in developing overall responses to all children in the local community. Their aim is that schools accommodate the widest range of diversity possible. In doing so they have evolved 'collaborative learning processes'. They state that this approach lies:

> in the capacity to merge the unique skills of talented adults and students, enfranchise team members through the participatory decision making process and distribute leadership authority beyond the administration to the broader school community.

They have been guided in this by the advice offered by Johnson and Johnson (1989) about cooperative group learning (equally applicable with adults or children). This approach involves:

- frequent face to face intervention – discussions between participants about the processes of learning;
- an 'all-for-one, one-for-all' feeling of positive interdependence;
- a focus on the development of group interpersonal skills;
- regular assessment of team functioning;
- methods of holding one another accountable for agreed commitments.

As Thousand and Villa state, this leads to a 'climate of equality and equity'. This surely must be a positive way to move towards valuing all contributions to the decision making processs, regardless of individuals' places in the hierarchy.

This collaborative approach also provides support systems for those involved. The process of change can be challenging, but the collaborative learning described involves the existence of the mutual support derived from working in the team. It is particularly important that this support exists when the work involves dealing with potential conflict.

I referred earlier to the power of learning in partnerships and the advantages this can bring. It seems to me that when assistants and teachers envisage training and staff development they mostly think of going out of school for courses. The most powerful form of staff development, which has an optimum impact on classroom practice, happens in those classrooms where two people consider classroom processes together. The fact that teachers and assistants have to work together in classrooms anyway, because of resource allocation, may be turned to great advantage. That is because looking at that existing partnership as an opportunity for staff development, while rethinking the task of sharing the classroom, is an opportunity to be capitalised on. It also deals in part with the training needs of teachers in terms of the management of assistants in their classrooms, which is clearly a matter of current concern, as I stated in Chapter 1. Of course, this class-based staff development is not the only solution, and opportunities outside the classroom where all the staff can discuss the development of their practice are important too. In addition training opportunities outside school for assistants should also be taken, where they are available and where assistants are able to pursue credit-bearing courses which lead to qualifications.

Reviewing practice and moving into action

In the activities in this book I have offered a framework for the review of practice in the school with regard to learning support assistants. This is based on the six principles outlined in Chapter 2. It follows the advice given by various authors and researchers on carrying out review procedures and offers the staff the opportunity to put forward their opinion on the school's practice. It is designed in such a way that it is likely to identify overall strengths already existing in the school's practice, while at the same time pinpointing weaknesses and areas for development. It also potentially highlights misperceptions or differences of opinion from individuals or groups about how effective the school is from their own particular perspective. It does this while protecting the anonymity of individuals.

Schools which have used the review framework have found it to be helpful as the results are made public and may become the focus of debate about the issues which are seen to be positive features, and may create a positive feeling about them. At the same time issues raised which suggest some action is needed can be considered. This discussion in itself provides a staff development forum, whether it is among small or larger groups of staff.

Having had this discussion it is then possible to identify an area on which some focused staff development work could be done. A strategy for this is also offered in the activities provided with advice on planning and moving into action. Of course, many schools are working to agreed action plans of other kinds, but the strategy offered here is reasonably simple, clear and usable by all participants, while asking a set of key questions which facilitate contextually related actions, particularly with respect to existing school systems and structures. These questions should be answered by both individuals and their team. A diagrammatic form, which can be filled in as a group response, having agreed a course of action, is also provided.

This form of action planning encourages the commitment of both individuals and teams to the decisions taken. It therefore helps to build in the 'positive interdependence' that Johnson and Johnson (1989) advise. In all these activities assistants are seen as equal group members with other members of staff. It identifies both actions for those other than the immediate group of people involved, and which among them might be responsible for involving those members of the wider school team; for example, heads of departments, headteacher, senior management, advisers, governors, parents, children and students might all be brought in at some stage. It also includes questions that ensure the group or team identifies realistic timescales for action, and plots dates and times for reviewing and monitoring progress either individually or together. From here the next stage may be embarked upon.

In conclusion

I now turn to the issue of making a decision about how wide the scope of the proposed developments might be. The coordinator of the development has to be aware of the necessity for a corporate decision to be carried out after reviewing practice in school. The group of people involved in this first review should be encouraged to consider and discuss the matter. The coordinator, having assimilated the notions and assumptions about the nature of collaborative inquiry offered here, should be in a position to facilitate this discussion.

Challenging the status quo may be the outcome of the team's decision. This can be an uncomfortable and difficult process and this should be acknowledged at the outset. However, if there is a commitment to collaborative learning, then the mutual support on offer to all members of the team should see them through bad patches. (Remember, the activities offer the option to plan for actions at either or both of two levels, after deciding on the scope of the planned development.) It may be useful here to consider the analogy of the root and the branch. It will be possible to make changes to twigs and branches without challenging wider attitudes, perceptions and practice in school. This in itself can benefit the immediate team and its practice. However, if the 'root' of the system remains the same, then there will be severe limitations on the school as a whole in its competency to develop its attitudes, ethos, policy, practice and provision for meeting the needs of a diverse range of children and students. Having said that, the most fundamental aspect of the development of schools that are effective in meeting the needs of all children is the way teachers and assistants together consider teaching and learning processes and the strategies used for the management of the classroom to support these. Again, it is the classroom and the adults who work in it that are in the forefront of development.

The challenge to the status quo is the basis of my 'author's health warning'. The process can be painful, but if acknowledged as a schoolwide issue the benefits can be many and positive. These benefits will be the development of the confidence and competence of teachers to engage in effective classroom partnerships with assistants, through managing their involvement well, and the enhanced skills of those assistants as they go about their work. The inclusion of the assistants in all of this work is underlined by the rationale for the six principles which are the basis of the activities, i.e. they are part of a team involved in a holistic learning process.

4 Organising collaborative enquiry

This chapter contains advice for the coordinator of the work in school. It consists of instructions on the use of the activity resources, how to run staff development sessions, in particular carrying out a review of practice and the process of action planning and other specific group processes. The coordinator is addressed as 'you' throughout the detailed instructions and the activities themselves.

The activities in Part Two of this book have been extensively tested in a range of contexts and schools. This experience indicates that care must be taken to create positive conditions for carrying out a collaborative inquiry. In more detail, the chapter contents which support the creation of these conditions are as follows:

1. General instructions on the use of the activities.
2. Practical advice on how to run the sessions, including:
   general advice
   preparation for sessions
   introductions to sessions
   group sizes
   timings
   ending of sessions
   planning/negotiating further sessions.
3. Instructions on how to carry out review of practice.
4. Instructions for action planning:
   questions to ask
   an outline
   planning - at what level?
   review of action.
5. Specific instructions on:
   Brainstorming
   Nominal Group Technique
   Brick Walls
   Poster Tour.
6. Conditions for success.

1. General instructions

The core and extension activities in this part of the book are intended for flexible use in any or all of the following ways:

- as a focus for a partnership discussion between teacher and assistant (level 1);
- as a focus for a small team or departmental meeting (level 1);
- in a series of individual workshops (level 1 and/or level 2);
- in staff development sessions, e.g. on professional development 'closure' days, for the whole school (level 1 and/or level 2);
- as a series of team development meetings over a period of time to be determined by the participants (level 1 and/or level 2);
- as a focus for staff development sessions to run concurrently with others above, but for the assistant group alone. NB These are *not* a substitute for joint teacher/assistant sessions.

Therefore, at their most intimate level some of the activities can be used by one teacher and one assistant as a minimum (producing a dialogue for staff development) although some activities would require a third party as a resource/observer. These smallest groups are coded with the symbols shown as: A, in the box below.

At the other end of the continuum many activities can be used by the whole school staff. These are coded with the symbols shown as: C, in the box below.

Most of them can be used by any sized group in between and are coded with the symbols shown as: B, in the box below.

Guidance is given on group sizes in each set of the various activities by the use of the above codes.

The core activities in each set are followed by extension activities under three headings:

Primary, coded with the symbols shown as: D, in the box below.

Secondary, coded: with the symbols shown as E, in the box below.

Assistants only groups, coded with the symbols shown as: F, in the box below.

These activities have been devised for use in the three different settings suggested. This means that they deal with situations that arise in those particular contexts more closely than those general and thematic ones found throughout the core activities. The primary and secondary activities are again split into level 1 and level 2, with action planning.

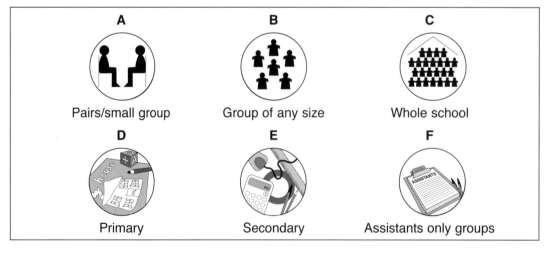

It is intended that whatever the size of the group it should include *at least one assistant*. This will provide support and staff development for assistants, and involve the assistants' perceptions, opinions, skills, ideas and actions in the team/staff development that results.

The activities should ideally be used in the following order:
1. Review of practice.
2. Choice of set to be used as a result of the review.
3. Use of action planning advice as a seminar for intended participants (if appropriate).
4. Use of the relevant set and part of that set suggested by the review of practice.
5. Action planning and developments.
6. Review of actions taken.

However, they are also designed to be very flexible; 'dipping in' to suit needs at a particular time, amending the text to suit the context, or a 'pick-and-mix' approach can also be helpful as needs for staff development arise. Whatever else, the process is the most important aspect and the inclusion of assistants within that process.

The process is underpinned by the Active Learning Framework, based on strategies included in the Teacher Education Resource Pack 'Special Needs in the Classroom' (Unesco 1991), and some core instructions on how the coordinator should lead sessions. The Active Learning Framework consists of a series of steps that form the basis of each of the activities, sometimes amended slightly but never left out:

1. Introduce the aims and topic	5 mins
2. Start with a review of individuals' personal experiences	5 mins
3. Share these with others	10 mins
4. Engage in problem solving activities	15 mins
5. Draw out some general principles and priorities	10 mins
6. Shape these into action plans and evaluation issues	10 mins
7. Individually reflect on learning and implications for own practice	5 mins

The suggested timings are for a one hour session, but this is only for guidance, and most of the activities will take at least an hour and a half. It is also important that you 'read' how various stages are going and adjust as you go along – flexibility in response to group needs is important. Make sure everyone has an individual time to reflect on their learning. This should *not* get left out.

If you wish to alter the text of the activity, or the timing, or split it into two sessions, for example, to make effective use of time, it is important to remember the framework steps, which should not be lost in any amendments made.

2. Advice on how to run the sessions

General advice

In carrying out the activities with your colleagues remember the notion of a collaborative inquiry.

Use the activity process sheets to support your facilitation of the activities and as prompts.

It is important to create a comfortable atmosphere for the sessions with appropriate accommodation and seating, but also through the 'climate' created in the group(s).

The coordinator should not be considered the 'fount of all knowledge'. In a collaborative inquiry everybody has something to offer which is worthwhile. You as coordinator are in a position to reflect back questions, drawing others in to see how they would answer the question that has been directed at you.

Having encouraged people's contributions, it is important to acknowledge them, particularly when they come from somebody who had to pluck up courage to respond.

Where there are continuous negative comments from one or more people in the group then the group should be encouraged to find strategies to overcome the 'ah buts...'. It may be possible to use the Brick Walls technique detailed on page 66 as a means of getting participants to think more positively about matters under consideration. This is also the main process used in set 3, level 2 of the core activities.

Preparation for the sessions

It is important to prepare the activity resources and the room to be used for the sessions, and to make sure the session will not be interrupted.

Adequate copies of all the activity resources should be prepared. It can be very unsettling for a group if the coordinator disappears in the middle of a session to photocopy frantically something forgotten, or to make more copies if there are not enough.

You may well find it worthwhile to conduct a short 'seminar' on the principles of action planning prior to using the sets of activities themselves, as it is a core process and, as such, very important. To do this, talking would-be participants through the activities and processes detailed in the latter part of this chapter would be helpful.

Making sure that you feel prepared yourself for the sessions is at least as important, if not more, than preparing others, and the resources. Be sure that you are comfortable about both the content and process issues with which you will be engaging, and your role in these. Spend time becoming very familiar with the activity process sheets, and possible timings.

It is best for you to be part of the group(s), not sitting apart as if you don't belong, unless the topic is better discussed by group members without you there; in a few instances this may be the case. However, mostly you will have a better insight into the issues if you do join the discussion, but of course it does mean that your own preparation must be thorough, so that you can be a group member and the group facilitator simultaneously.

Introduction to the sessions

State or restate the aims for the session, as written in the activities.

If there is any possibility that you have people in the group who do not know one another, make sure introductions are done. This is not impossible, particularly if you are working at whole school level in a big school, or there are new members of staff.

Be clear at the start how long the session will last.

Group sizes

Details about the size and type of group are given in coded logo form on the activities.

If people are somewhat reticent to volunteer comments in the big group it is generally better to get people to 'chat with a neighbour/partner' first of all, then perhaps in fours, before the whole group attempts discussion.

You will find it useful to allow for this within the timescale for the programme, so that people do have an opportunity to chat in a non-threatening way.

Timings

Timings should be devised as proportions of the overall activity, as the length of each one will vary. However, each one should be at least an hour, and many of them would benefit from an hour and a half. Some need two hours to be done thoroughly, particularly those involving a large whole group.

Of course, you have to work within the timescales you have available to you, but as a rough guide, the less attention paid to working an activity through properly, the less effective will be the outcomes.

If for any reason you have to alter the overall length of the session, or split it into two shorter sessions, keep the proportions for the activity similar to those suggested in the 'active learning framework' for an hour's session.

Stick to the time stated and agreed at the outset, even if, as the session goes on, people seem to be very engaged with the tasks. They may well be, but would still wish to finish at the agreed time, and it is your responsibility to make sure this happens.

Ending the sessions

Where a debrief is suggested, make sure that it has taken place. Sometimes it is worth finishing the activity itself quite early in order to debrief more fully, and summarise the agreed actions clearly once more. These reflections on the learning that has taken place, and on the implications of that learning, are important for individual participants and the group as a whole.

Finish on time – don't risk alienating people, or abusing their own time.

Planning and negotiating future sessions

Guidance on this is given in the sets of activities and the action planning guidelines.

However, having the group together is an ideal opportunity to set dates, and much better than attempting to do it piecemeal or through memos afterwards, so it is worth stressing that it is better to incorporate it into the session, where possible, rather than being tempted to leave it.

3. Instructions on the review of practice

Review of practice

In order to carry out a review of current or existing practice in the school you may find it helpful to use the review schedule offered below. It may of course be amended for use as a discussion or interview document to take account of school circumstances, rather than as a questionnaire for carrying out a whole school survey.

A more sophisticated version of this review can be developed through the use of a detailed questionnaire which seeks more illumination into certain aspects of the school's practice. This can follow the format below but in addition ask for clarification on certain issues in a more open-ended way.

For example, questions aimed more specifically at classroom practice, with specific questions for teachers and assistants that are pertinent to their individual and joint responsibilities, might be helpful. Incorporated into the teachers' schedule might be the following examples:

- Do you feel comfortable with an assistant working in the classroom?
- Do you build their 'time' into your planning? In what ways?

In the assistants' version there might be the following:

- Do you think the teaching staff are aware of your capabilities and interests in the classroom with the children? Give an example.
- Are teachers' expectations of you realistic?

4. Action planning

Moving into action – general points

The resources for action planning can be used flexibly to suit the school's and individuals' needs. You may find it useful to provide a seminar for the people you expect to be involved in using the sets of activities. This seminar could take the form of a discussion about the process of action planning, for example. You should guide the participants through the action planning questions and the process, encouraging questions and clarification of the process.

Review Schedule

In which areas of our team's/department's/school's practice are we doing well?
In which areas could some improvement be made?

For each of these six statements of principle, please ring the rating scale, which ranges from [1] needs little or no improvement to [6] needs a great deal of improvement.

Learning support assistants should:

1. be clear about their roles and responsibilities   1   2   3   4   5   6

2. be included in and understand the communication
   system in the school   1   2   3   4   5   6

3. be seen positively as part of the provision to meet
   children's and students' educational needs   1   2   3   4   5   6

4. be part of a working team   1   2   3   4   5   6

5. be encouraged to make use of their personal and
   professional skills   1   2   3   4   5   6

6. be supported in the development of their
   professional skills   1   2   3   4   5   6

Please hand in to ....

by ....

Thank you. Your answers will contribute to an overall picture, and you will not be identified individually within that.

Action planning questions

As a group or individually you will find it helpful to answer the following questions in the order suggested:

What do you intend to do now (short term objective)?
- as individuals?
- as pairs/partnerships?
- as teachers?
- as assistants?
- as a team?

Why do you intend to do it? (Don't miss out this question, it is vitally important: if someone else asks you why you are proposing this course of action it will prepare you and your colleagues to answer clearly.)

How do you intend to do it?
- contact?
- discussion?
- meetings?
- in-service sessions?

Who do you intend to involve in it?
- just yourselves?
- others, e.g. senior management/head/governors/other colleagues/ pupils/parents/INSET coordinator/LEA staff/other professionals?

By when do you intend to have achieved
- your shorter term objectives?

How will you know you have achieved them? What are the criteria/ indicators?

When will you review and evaluate?

Who will
- monitor and review?
- evaluate?

How will they evaluate? Remember, it is important to
- state why you propose to take the actions you are planning;
- keep your timescale realistic;
- put a review/evaluation procedure into place, both ongoing and summative; and
- give everyone involved or affected a copy of the finalised version.

Action planning: levels 1 and 2

Do you wish (as a group) to attempt the kinds of activities aimed at level 1 – a review and development of practice, as suggested by your activity outlines? If 'yes', then level 1 action planning deals with smaller scale developments in practice within present agreed school policy. This does not preclude working at level 2 sometime in the future.

Action planning outline

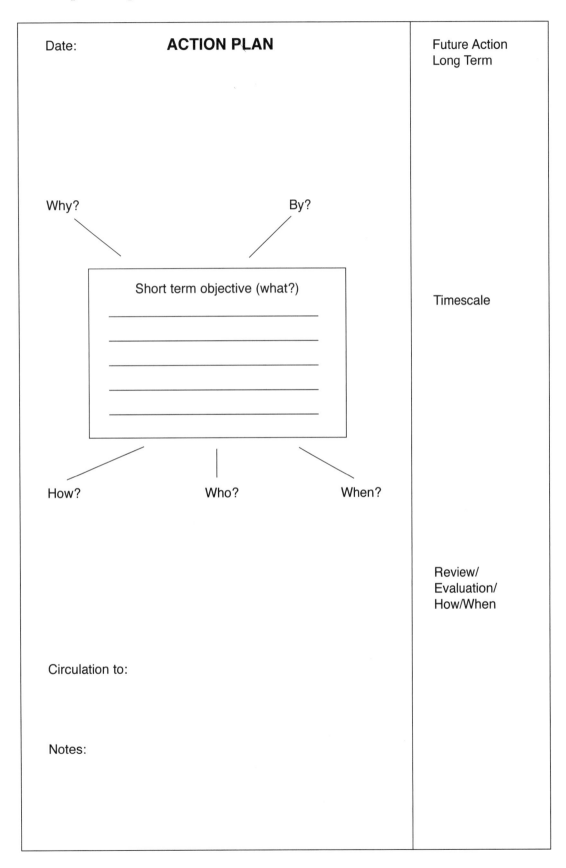

ACTION PLAN

Date:

Future Action
Long Term

Why?   By?

Short term objective (what?)

Timescale

How?   Who?   When?

Review/
Evaluation/
How/When

Circulation to:

Notes:

The issues you have identified as a result of your activities from the first section of your chosen set of activities may suggest to you that action planning on a small scale will not be sufficient. To be addressed in enough depth a review of school policy with regard to those issues may well be helpful.

The following questions might help you to draw up an interim plan to facilitate the move into level 2 action, using the activities in the second section of the set on which you have been working:

- Do you wish to use the activities in level 2? These address wider issues to do with whole-school approaches and policy.
- How will you (as a coordinator, or as a group) organise time and space to do it?
- When will you be doing the organising? How will you do it?
- Indeed, can you do it?
- Does it necessitate senior management/headteacher's backing to do it? It may well do so, as it is aimed at more fundamental issues than level 1.
- How would you expect them to back you, in principle and/or at a practical level – in the form of time/resources?
- Should this proposed action go into the school development plan? If so, how will it get there?
- How realistic is the timescale you are about to set yourself?
- What else may compete with what you want to do?

You may also find it useful to refer to Fullan and Park's (1981) advice about whether the school is ready for this kind of action at this point; how receptive it might be to change and its implementation. West and Ainscow's (1991) version of Fullan and Park describes implementation as 'the process of altering existing practice in order to achieve more effectively certain desired outcomes for pupils'.

According to Fullan and Park (1981) four themes seem to be especially critical. Consider these with respect to your own development plans:

1. the nature of change itself;
2. characteristics of the school system;
3. characteristics of the school and the people who work in it;
4. external factors.

A consideration of the advice on change processes and their relationship to school structures and cultures may be found in Fullan (1995), and Ainscow *et al.* (1994a), if you feel that you wish to consult theoretical and research sources for advice on managing the change process in schools.

Reviewing the action

Some questions for consideration:

As a group remind yourselves of your immediate objective(s) and why you decided on that course of action.

Individually review your own particular responsibility within the plan and what happened.

Consider why it happened:
- What helped progress?
- What hindered progress?

As a group consider your collaborative plan of action:
- What happened? Why?
- What helped/hindered?
- Were there any unintended outcomes? If so, what were they?
- Do you need to redraw the action plan?

If so, go back to the original questions:
- Why? What? How? Who? When?
- How will we monitor/evaluate?

If you do not need to redraw it and are satisfied with progress and developments made, set a date to review this. Then, you will need to ask:
- Has progress been maintained?
- If so, how?
- Has improvement in practice been maintained?
- If so, in what ways?

5. Specific instructions

Brainstorming

This approach is useful in creating an agenda for discussion within the group. The procedure is as follows.

For a set period (about ten minutes) participants offer ideas, suggestions or comments related to the issue under consideration. One of the group members records the contributions, preferably onto a flipchart, blackboard or overhead projector, so all can see them. In order that *all* participants feel confident to offer ideas without fear of criticism, it is *essential* that they follow strictly these rules:

- All ideas related to the issues in any direct way are accepted.
- The maximum number of related ideas is expected.
- One idea may be modified, adapted or expressed as another idea.
- Ideas should be expressed in a clear and concise manner.
- No discussion of the ideas is allowed; it must not be attempted.
- There must be *no* criticism of ideas.

Once the list has been gathered, at the end of the brainstorming period, the agenda for normal discussion is ready.

Nominal group technique

A method of obtaining group responses to questions or problems which:

- ensures that everybody contributes;
- avoids the dominance of the group by a few people with strong ideas;
- avoids too narrow an interpretation of the task;
- ensures a wide variety of responses;
- allows a systematic ordering of priorities.

The procedure is as follows:

Clarification of the task

The task is presented on a blackboard, flipchart or overhead projector, e.g. 'How can the school's communication system be improved?' In order that all participants fully understand the question, time is spent in group discussion about the nature of the task.

Silent nominations

Individuals are given a fixed period to list their own private responses. This should not be hurried. They are then asked to rank their own list in order to establish felt priorities.

Master list

The group leader compiles a master list on the blackboard, flipchart or overhead projector taking only one item from each group member in rotation. No editing of the material is allowed and no evaluating comments are to be made at this stage. It is helpful to number the items.

Item clarification

During this phase each item is discussed until all members know what it means. Clarification only is allowed. If a member of the group now feels their item is already covered by someone else's, they may request its withdrawal. No pressure should be applied to any individual to have items withdrawn or incorporated into another.

Evaluation

It is now necessary to decide the relative importance of items in the eyes of the group. Each person is allowed five weighted votes, i.e. five points for the item that is felt to be most important, four points for the next, and so on. A simple voting procedure allows the consensus to emerge.

Once the composite picture has emerged, it provides an agenda for normal group discussions to proceed.

Reminder to group leaders:

- Do not reinterpret a person's ideas.
- Use the participant's own wording.
- Do not interject your own ideas – *you* are not participating.
- Give people time to think.
- This is *not* a debate – do not allow participants to challenge each other or attempt to persuade each other.
- Do not try to interpret results – do not look for patterns.

Brick walls

This approach is particularly useful when considering how to implement a plan, or when considering the question 'What gets in the way of me/us reaching the desired objective?' The procedure is as follows.

In pairs or small groups there is discussion to consider how the bricks in the way might be removed, by either individual or team effort. Participants may also be asked to think whether any of the 'blocks' are of their own making.

At a group level, each person may offer one of their individual 'blocks' to a 'group brick wall' with a team or group objective to achieve. Then the group can discuss strategies for removing the bricks that are in the way, by either individual or team efforts. Consideration may also be given to acknowledging that at a certain stage some of the bricks are 'beyond our control'. This invites concentration in a positive way on the ones that can and should be removed in order to make progress towards the agreed objective.

Poster tour

The advantage of this activity process and debrief is that all people in the group have an accountability to learn what has been important in their group discussion, and to impart this to others in the large group. It also saves lengthy central debriefs by 'group spokespersons' when the whole group is a large one.

Small groups are formed; the outcomes of their discussions are displayed on large flipchart sheets and posted on the wall. The posters are spaced evenly round the room, not closely together.

The groups are re-formed so that there is a representative for each poster in each of these groups.

These new groups then move round the room, at intervals to suit how much time there is, perhaps up to five minutes, pausing at each poster while the group receives an explanation about each poster by that poster's representative in the group. Other group members can ask questions about the poster, and discussions and comparisons are facilitated.

It is advisable for the groups to move to each poster in an orderly fashion, for example all moving clockwise, so that everyone can be sure of seeing all of them.

6. Conditions for success

In order to carry out successful collaborative inquiry it is worth remembering that the following conditions are important:

- a genuinely collaborative atmosphere;
- trusting conditions;
- an acceptance of the worth of everybody's contribution;
- an agreed agenda for discussion and development and/or change;
- individual needs and contributions considered as part of the whole
- a sense of being accountable to one another;
- a commitment to work together as adult learners in order to enhance the learning environment for all the children and students in the school.

Part 2

STAFF DEVELOPMENT MATERIALS

ROLES AND RESPONSIBILITIES

Learning support assistants should be clear about their roles and responsibilities

AIM
To develop an understanding of the necessity for a relevant job description. This should ensure that assistants and other staff are clear about their roles and responsibilities.

PIGGY IN THE MIDDLE
Cameo: An assistant describes her lack of guidance:

> Nobody had explained to me properly what I'm supposed to do. I've been picking it up as I go along. Sometimes, but not regularly, I'm given instructions at the start of the day. And I haven't got a proper job description, only a vague one I got with my contract, it's not much practical use. Nobody refers to it anyway, and it's been like this for nearly four terms now.

ACTIVITY
Individually: Consider the following questions:
   What do you think has happened here?
   What do you think are the possible causes of the situation described?

As a group:
   Share your ideas.
   Make sure everyone has a turn.

Individually or in pairs: Consider how this compares with or differs from your own experience or that of your team?

As a group:
1. Discuss briefly these personal experiences in your school.
2. Think about the following questions:
   Why did it happen here?
   How did I feel about it?
   What did I/those involved do about it?
   How might I/those involved have dealt with it differently?

As a whole group:
1. Share these ideas.
2. List the causes as you see them on a flipchart.
3. Consider:
   Which of these could be avoided in the future?
   How might I/we go about preventing them?
4. Prioritise some ideas for action.

Coordinator: refer here to the guidance on writing out an action plan at level 1 or moving to level 2.

Now draw up your action plan.

When doing so think of the issues you have brought out through your discussions with regard to your assistants' job descriptions:

- Have they got job descriptions?
- When were they last referred to/reviewed?
- Are the assistants in any way involved in the drawing up or review of job descriptions?
- Was there an appraisal session (formal/informal)?

Use your outline sheet to help you as individuals to contribute to the whole group plan.

Roles and Responsibilities

ROLES AND RESPONSIBILITIES

Learning support assistants should be clear about their roles and responsibilities

AIM
To develop an understanding of the need to review practice in any classroom or situation where assistants are involved. Reviewing the role and responsibilities in this way helps to clarify what is working well and why this is so.

PIGGY IN THE MIDDLE
Cameo: A teacher, referring to assistants:

> Why should *we* spend time thinking about learning support assistants? Surely that's the job of the coordinator for special needs isn't it? – not us!

ACTIVITY
Individually: Bearing in mind the comment above:

- Review a recent and typical working week in your school/classroom.
- Think of a lesson/session when you share a classroom with another adult (teacher or assistant), and write some notes about what each person did in that lesson.

In pairs: Discuss what you have on your lists.

As a group:
You will need a person to take notes for the group and a spokesperson:

1. List all the types of activity which the assistant has been involved in during each stage of the lesson.
2. Think of the steps taken beforehand in preparation for these joint activities and list them.
3. How well did both the preparation and the activities themselves fit into the assistant's job description? Mark items which have direct relevance for planning and reviewing the role of the assistant.
4. How clear in each set of activities was the role of the assistant to either or both of the pair?

As a whole group:
1. Listen to the others' feedback.
2. Now you have reviewed your working practice, are there times in the future when you would see a need to review it again:
   - in pairs (classroom sharers)?
   - in team groups?
   - as a whole staff?
3. What actions will people now take as a result?

Now draw up your action plan.

Refer to the above questions and the issues you have identified in order to do this.

Use your outline sheet to help you as individuals to contribute to the whole.

You may find the attached aide memoire helpful as you plan.

AIDE MEMOIRE FOR PLANNING

In your planning together you need to take account of the following wherever possible:

- developing a joint understanding of the aims for the lesson/session and its place in the overall syllabus/module/curriculum
- defining the aims for the assistant's involvement at each stage of the session
- clarifying the respective responsibilities of each person in the session
- dealing with issues of discipline
- dealing with issues of safety
- considering contact with the teacher and the opportunity for full curriculum access for *all* the pupils in the group
- considering *all* the pupils' access to their peers as a source of support and learning
- preparing materials – who does what and why
- considering how all the pupils should relate to the respective adults and how they will be informed of/involved in this.

During the session(s) the assistant might well be:

- working to an agreed aim or set of aims for different stages of lesson
- making observational notes on pupils' responses to the tasks set as part of the assessment procedure
- particularly observing process – *how* pupils tackle/complete tasks
- working as a facilitator for any pupil needing support
- working with a specified group of targeted pupils
- using prepared/differentiated materials and assessing their effectiveness.

After the session(s):
1. Debrief the agreed aims for the session and for the assistant's involvement.
2. Considering these questions:

- Were there any notable unintended outcomes?
- What will happen next time?

NB This is an aide memoire, not a comprehensive set of instructions. You will need to develop additional ideas for your own context.

ROLES AND RESPONSIBILITIES

AIM

To consider in more detail current practice in the primary school classroom through planning some staff development, to take place in the classroom, related to the partnership of assistant and teacher. This should lead to the development of effective collaboration in practice.

ACTIVITY

Sharing classrooms and learning to develop the partnership

In pairs:

Think of a specific lesson/series of lessons between now and the next meeting of this pair/group when you know you will be sharing a classroom with each other/ another assistant or teacher. Write down some action points in response to considering the following questions:

- Why will we be working together in this situation?
- How will I/we prepare for the session(s)?
- What new or different strategy might we use?
- How will the children be prepared for the fact that we will be working together (differently)?
- How will our joint aims be clarified?
- What will each of us do at different points/stages in the session(s)?
- How will the activities be recorded?
- How will we know if our aims have been achieved?
- What is our timescale?

ACTION POINTS:
REFLECTION AND EVALUATION SESSION FOR A STAFF GROUP TO SHARE EXPERIENCES

In pairs/groups:

Each person briefly explain what you attempted to do, what was new or different about it, and why you tried it.

Then consider the following questions:

- Did the new action points work?
- Why?
- What difficulties did you encounter?
- What strategies did you use to overcome these?
- Would you do it again/incorporate it into your normal practice?
- If so, why? How?

Be ready to feed back main points of importance to the group.

Individually: reflect on what you have learnt from colleagues about their experiences and what might be significant for your own practice.

Help in the Classroom

ROLES AND RESPONSIBILITIES

Review sheet and planning activity for developing guidelines (based on aide memoire agenda) towards consistency in the school

AIM
To plan and review in the whole staff group developments made in classroom collaboration and practice.

CORE ISSUES TO CONSIDER:

- joint understanding of aims for a lesson/series of lessons and their place in the overall curriculum;
- aims for assistants' involvement;
- respective responsibilities of each adult in the session;
- dealing with issues of discipline/safety;
- curriculum access for *all* children (through teacher/materials/activities);
- *all* children's access to working with peers at some stage or all of the lesson;
- preparation of materials;
- how all children should relate to the respective adults – how they are to be informed of/involved in this.

Additional issues for this session (add more of your own that have arisen during activities):

- groups/grouping/individual targets
- physical layout of classroom
- required knowledge, skills, experience of each adult
- recording of processes
- recording of learning outcomes (yours as well as children's!).

REVIEW OF ACTIVITIES *AFTER* THEIR TRIAL IN CLASSROOMS

Individually:
Reflect on the activities you tried from your own perspective.

In pairs:
1. Debrief the aims:
    for adults
    for children
    for lesson(s).
2. Consider approaches to:
    classroom organisation
    observations made
    classroom processes
    outcomes – intended/unintended
    target achievements.

Whole group:
Consider these questions:

- What will happen next time?
- What has been learnt at a whole school level?
- Can we now draw up school guidelines using our reflection and review of these activities?

ROLES AND RESPONSIBILITIES

AIM

To consider in more detail current practice in the secondary school classroom through planning some staff development, to take place in the classroom, related to the partnership of assistant and teacher. This should lead to the development of effective collaboration in practice.

ACTIVITY

Sharing classrooms and learning to develop the partnership

In pairs

Think of a specific lesson/series of lessons between now and the next meeting of this pair/group when you know you will be sharing a classroom with each other/another assistant or teacher. Write down some action points in response to considering the following questions:

- Why will we be working together in this situation?
- How will I/we prepare for the session(s)?
- What new or different strategy might I/we use?
- How will the students be prepared for the fact that we will be working together (differently)?
- How will our joint aims be clarified?
- What will each of us do at different points/stages in the session(s)?
- How will the activities be recorded?
- How will we know if our aims have been achieved?
- What is our timescale?

ACTION POINTS:

-
-
-
-
-
-
-

Roles and Responsibilities

REFLECTION AND EVALUATION SESSION FOR A STAFF GROUP TO SHARE EXPERIENCES

In pairs/groups:

1. Each person briefly explain what you attempted to do, what was new or different about it, and why you tried it.
2. Consider the following questions:
   Did the new action points work?
   Why?
   What difficulties did you encounter?
   What strategies did you use to overcome these?
   Would you do it again/incorporate it into your normal practice?
   If so, why? How?

Be ready to feedback main points of importance to the group.

Individually: reflect on what you have learnt from colleagues about their experiences and what might be significant for your own practice in classroom collaboration.

ROLES AND RESPONSIBILITIES

REVIEW SHEET AND PLANNING ACTIVITY FOR DEVELOPING GUIDELINES (BASED ON AIDE MEMOIRE AGENDA) TOWARDS CONSISTENCY IN THE SCHOOL.

AIM
To plan and review in the whole staff group developments made in classroom collaboration and practice.

CORE ISSUES TO CONSIDER:

- previous information for assistant on curriculum/module content;
- joint understanding of aims for a lesson/series of lessons and their place in the overall curriculum;
- aims for assistant's involvement;
- respective responsibilities of each adult in the session;
- dealing with issues of discipline/safety;
- curriculum access for *all* students (through teacher/materials/activities);
- *all* students' access to working with peers at some stage or all of the lesson;
- preparation of materials;
- negotiation with students about appropriate strategies/levels of independence.

Additional issues for this session (add more of your own that have arisen during activities):

- groups/grouping/individual targets
- physical layout of classroom
- required knowledge, skills, experience of each adult
- particular curriculum subject requirements
- recording of processes
- recording of learning outcomes (yours as well as students'!).

REVIEW OF ACTIVITIES *AFTER* THEIR TRIAL IN CLASSROOMS

Individually:
Reflect on the activities you tried from your own perspective.

In pairs:
1. Debrief the aims:
   - for adults
   - for students
   - for lesson(s).
2. Consider approaches to:
   - classroom organisation
   - observations made
   - classroom processes
   - outcomes – intended/unintended
   - target achievements.

Whole group:

- What will happen next time?
- What has been learnt at a whole school level?
- Can we now draw up school guidelines using our reflection and review of these activities?

Roles and Responsibilities

ROLES, RESPONSIBILITIES AND RELATIONSHIPS

AIM

To explore and analyse aspects of the assistant's role in such ways that feelings of reward, challenge and stress are identified and the sources of those feelings are located. Through this activity it is then possible to identify courses of action that may be taken in respect of the assistants' roles and relationships in the school, by the assistants themselves, by them and close colleagues and by members of the wider school team.

ACTIVITY

Rewards, challenges and stresses

Individually:

- On three separate pieces of paper headed 'Rewarding', 'Challenging', 'Stressful', write brief notes from your particular personal perspective on what you feel in experiencing the rewarding, challenging and stressful aspects of your role. Try not to discuss it with colleagues yet; make your notes alone, so they reflect your own individual point of view and experiences.

With a partner:

- Share your ideas with each other about each of the three aspects in turn.
- Consider the reasons behind them.

In three groups (of six or nine):

- Collect all the papers from all group members under each of the three headings so that each group can analyse all responses to 'rewarding', or 'challenging', or 'stressful' aspects of the role.
- Each group should analyse their data and make a 'master list' which contains all the examples from each group member, marking any that occur more than once, and checking that no items are missing from this master list.
- Below this add organising headings that reflect the reasons for, or sources of, the feelings expressed. These might, for example, be timetabling constraints; job description issues; relationships with an individual child or member of staff or parent; own strengths or lack of confidence. There will be many more sources – these are ideas to get you going with the analysis.
- Record on the master list in a clear way what you have identified.
- Be ready to feed back to the whole group what you have found.

As a whole group:

1. Record onto a flipchart your examples and analysis from each group of the major themes under the three headings, rewarding, challenging and stressful.
2. Think of how you can build on rewarding features, meet challenges and relieve stresses.
3. Identify some action points that are within your individual control and prioritise one or two of them.
4. Then identify some action points that you and a close colleague or small team might take and prioritise one or two.
5. Then identify and prioritise some action points for members of the wider school team, including management, and identify who might have some control over getting something to happen.

Individually:

Identify:

- what you have learnt;
- what is positive about your work;
- what potential actions you have thought of that you can do something about;
- who might help you with these;
- how long, realistically, they will take;
- how you will review these activities;
- how other colleagues can help you to review them; and
- when reviewing can take place.

Roles and Responsibilities

COMMUNICATION

Learning support assistants should be included in and understand the communication system of the school

AIM
To consider how well the assistants can be involved in the communication system of the school, and to develop an understanding of the necessity for this.

NO-MAN'S-LAND
Cameo: An assistant describes a breakdown in communication:

I only found out yesterday that Mrs P was leaving next Friday. It was really embarrassing because I know *now* that she has to go because the devolved budget isn't enough to pay for everything. I really put my foot in it yesterday. I asked her about who she would be working with next term – it might have been me. She was feeling pretty down about it – and *I* didn't help!

The one good thing about it is, the deputy head's agreed that there should be a list of the main points from the business staff meeting, so that those of us who only work half days, or are ill or something, won't miss out on that kind of news again.

ACTIVITY
Individually:
Think about this assistant's description of what happened to her. Consider other ways in which she might have been embarrassed or put in a difficult situation by missing out on information; draw on your own experience here.

As a group:
1. Brainstorm any ways in which you think a similar situation could arise in your school.
2. List these on a flipchart.
3. List any gaps you perceive in the communication system of the school as they pertain to you. (Assistants, be *very* honest here!)
4. Explore possible strategies to avoid these gaps.
5. List these on a flipchart.
6. Prioritise them in a way which suits you as a group.

Here are two suggestions (you may prefer something different):

either those which would be easy to avoid by taking minimal action for immediate results;
or those which you feel would avoid the worst potential incidences, particularly for assistants, by taking action.

Coordinator:
Refer here to the guidance on working out an action plan at level 1 or moving to level 2.

Now draw up your action plan
When doing so think of the priorities you have identified during your discussions, and how actions you can take individually or together might lead to better communication. Consider:

- Can you plug any identified gaps and if so, how?
- How can any other improvements be made?
- What are the good areas of the communication system? Can we extend them?

COMMUNICATION

Learning support assistants should be included in and understand the communication system of the school

AIM
To examine the school's communication system with particular respect to the role of the learning support assistant.

NO-MAN'S-LAND
Cameo: An assistant describes an unfortunate incident:

> Sometimes we are in a really difficult position. It's about 'officialdom' – where does it end? How much should I say or should the teacher say? A parent was in the other day – she more or less pinned me up against the wall, and insisted on me giving her some information. I didn't know enough about it, but wasn't sure whether to tell her or not anyway. She didn't seem to realise that it was perhaps the head's job to do this – she also said 'Well, who are you, if you can't tell me?' So I explained . . . it was *really* embarrassing!

ACTIVITY
As a group:
> Tease out the issues that underly this somewhat complex and embarrassing situation.
> Who should have known about what?
> Why do you think they didn't?

Individually:
> Think of experiences/situations in your school which have any similarities to the one above.

As a group:
Using the Nominal Group Technique consider the following question: How can the school's communication system be improved?

You will then be able to identify priorities for action.

Now draw up your action plan.

Using the priorities identified from your master list, and keeping in mind both:

- what assistants should know; and
- what others should know about them.

you can now plan your way ahead.

Communication

COMMUNICATION

MEMO RESPONSE ACTIVITY A

AIM
To consider issues of communication in a school as they affect assistants, through a memo response activity. The real examples, actual memos written by assistants in primary schools, stimulate discussion and problem solving through both seeking strategies to ease the difficulties described or prevent them arising, and relating these ideas to your own school context.

Individually:
Read the memo you have.
Write some notes as to what you see to be the implications.
Notes

In pairs:
Discuss your individual reactions to the memo.
Think of some responses and strategies to resolve the problems described.
Notes

Be ready to share your ideas with the rest of the group.

As a whole group:
1. List strategies discussed by the pairs on a flipchart.
2. Mark any of them that seem to have relevance for your school context.
3. Write some action points for individuals, pairs and bigger groups to take.

Individually:
Reflect on your personal situation. What have you learnt about your own communication skills and the situations in which you find yourself?

MEMO FOR RESPONSE
ACTIVITY A

Level 1

MEMO TO THE CLASS TEACHER(S)

Something I'd like to change about my work is the poor attitude of others towards all support staff, and to be appreciated by you and acknowledged for the work I do with the children.

Because you seem to be resentful and unappreciative of the work I encourage the children to do, and confidence is lost. However, greater responsibility is still expected to be taken for less reward.

Something I'd like to learn more about is all aspects of teaching through more in-house school training.

Because I would like to become more involved.

What I like best about my work is the children's response to me.

--------------------------------✂--------------------------------

Level 2

MEMO TO THE HEADTEACHER/MANAGEMENT OF THE SCHOOL

Something I'd like to change about my work is to be given time with the staff on a weekly basis to discuss plans/lessons etc. for the coming week.

Because I find it difficult for the class teacher and myself to plan accordingly in a few minutes before each session in front of (by this time) a disrupted class of children.

Something I'd like to learn more about is how to deal with bad behaviour in school.

Because I sometimes feel I deal with it in the wrong way.

The way I'd like to do it is to do a course.

What I like best about my work is working as a team.

Communication

COMMUNICATION

MEMO RESPONSE ACTIVITY B

AIM

To consider issues of communication in a school as they affect assistants, through a memo response activity. The real examples, actual memos written by assistants in primary schools, stimulate discussion and problem solving through both seeking strategies to ease the difficulties described or prevent them arising, and relating these to your own school. Drawing up some pointers or guidelines together as a whole staff group will support the development of more consistent communications in the school.

Individually:
Read the memo you have.
Write some notes as to what you see to be the implications.
Notes

In pairs:
Discuss your individual reactions to the memo.
Think of some responses and strategies to resolve the problems described.
Notes

Be ready to share your ideas with the rest of the group.

As a whole group:
1. List strategies discussed by the pairs on a flipchart.
2. Mark any of them that seem to have relevance for your school context.
3. Write some action points for individuals, pairs and bigger groups to take.
4. Draw up some pointers or guidelines, which are inclusive and involving of assistants in particular that would contribute to improved communication systems in the school. Make sure that individual and joint accountabilities are built in through an agreed review procedure, with a realistic timescale.

Individually:
• Reflect on your own commitments within these plans. What have you learnt?

Help in the Classroom

COMMUNICATION

MEMO RESPONSE ACTIVITY C

AIM

To consider issues of communication in a school as they affect assistants, through a memo response activity. The real examples, actual memos written by assistants in secondary schools, stimulate discussion and problem solving both through seeking strategies to ease the difficulties described or prevent them arising, and in relating these ideas to your own school context.

Individually:
Read the memo you have.
Write some notes as to what you see to be the implications.
Notes

In pairs:
Discuss your individual reactions to the memo.
Think of some responses and strategies to resolve the problems described.
Notes

Be ready to share your ideas with the rest of the group.

As a whole group:
1. List strategies discussed by the pairs on a flipchart.
2. Mark any of them that seem to have relevance for your school context.
3. Write some action points for individuals, pairs and bigger groups to take.

Individually:
Reflect on your personal situation. What have you learnt about your own communication skills and the situations in which you find yourself?

Communication

MEMO FOR RESPONSE
ACTIVITY C

Set 1 Level 1

MEMO TO THE CLASS TEACHERS I WORK WITH

Something I'd like to change about my work is to have time to communicate with each of you, e.g. on the subject of the lesson; what you want me to do during the lesson; time to tell you how the students have performed; level of support given.

Because I would then know whether I am doing my job correctly; if not, where can I improve my performance, e.g. did your lesson go as planned with me in your classroom? If not, how can we improve?

Something I'd like to learn more about is the planning of lessons.

Because I would like to prepare myself for the subject being taught.

What I like best about my work is the rewards of working with the students.

--%<--

Set 2 Level 2

MEMO TO THE HEADTEACHER/SENIOR MANAGEMENT TEAM

Something I'd like to change about my work is the attitude of some teachers to my presence in class, plus the lack of information about the planned lessons.

Because going in blind to some lessons is very disconcerting and disorientating and hampers my ability to help the students who need it.

Something I'd like to learn more about is IT, as it is becoming a more important part of education.

Because at present I am way out of my depth with regard to it and am unable to be much, if any, help.

The way I'd like to learn about it is on an out-of-school course, because there will be no way that you can be distracted by being called away for a work-related reason.

What I like best about my work is the sense of achievement when you have helped a student to understand and do a task they were thought of as never being able to grasp or understand.

Help in the Classroom

COMMUNICATION

MEMO RESPONSE ACTIVITY D

AIM

To consider issues of communication in a school as they affect assistants, through a memo response activity. The real examples, actual memos written by assistants in secondary schools, stimulate discussion and problem solving both through seeking strategies to ease the difficulties described or prevent them arising, and relating these to your own school. Drawing up some pointers or guidelines together as a whole staff group will support the development of more consistent communications in the school.

Individually:
Read the memo you have.
Write some notes as to what you see to be the implications.
Notes

In pairs, small groups:
Discuss your individual reactions to the memo.
Think of some responses and strategies to resolve the problems described.
Notes

Be ready to share your ideas with the rest of the group.
As a whole group:
1. List strategies discussed by the small groups on a flipchart.
2. Mark any of them that seem to have relevance for your school context.
3. Write some action points for individuals, pairs, subject departments, year groups and bigger groups to take.
4. Draw up some pointers or guidelines, which are inclusive and involving of assistants in particular that would contribute to improved communication systems in the school. Make sure that individual and joint accountabilities are built in through an agreed review procedure, with a realistic timescale.

Individually:
Reflect on your own commitments within these plans. What have you learnt?
What are the implications for your own context, e.g. subject department, class partnership?

Communication

COMMUNICATION

MEMO RESPONSE ACTIVITY E

AIM
To explore assistants' current experiences of communication in the school through the use of a memo exercise. By discussing what they have written and ways of approaching the issues described the assistants have an opportunity to develop ideas about how to deal personally with some of the concerns they face in their particular role and context. [The information generated may be used (anonymously) for the activities with teaching staff in the preceding four activities, instead of the examples offered there.] Using samples of the stimulus material on OHPs will help to generate ideas.

Individually:
Complete the memo outline using your own current concerns – you will be talking to other assistants about it and they may read it later.

Explore each aspect – the positive features and the difficulties you face in your work. In particular, think of the things you need to know or skills and knowledge you want to develop. You may find the examples on the OHPs stimulate your thinking.

In pairs/small groups:
Tell/show each other what you have written and why.

Using the outline analysis sheet develop some ideas about how you and others in the school might or should respond to the issues discussed.

As a whole group:
Discuss some of the issues raised.
Consider these questions:

- What can assistants individually or together do to raise these issues or bring about developments for themselves?
- Who should they approach in order to communicate them?
- In what ways should they go about it?
- Who might they ask to be an advocate to communicate with others on their behalf?
- What is 'beyond assistants' immediate control' and will need action on the part of others in the school?

Individually:
Reflect on what you have learnt about your own communication skills.
Think about whether you feel more confident in expressing opinions, concerns and needs as a result of this activity. Who will you be speaking to and what will you say?

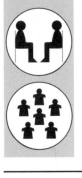

Help in the Classroom

MEMO FOR RESPONSE
ACTIVITY E

Memo to: class teacher(s) with whom I work most often*
or: headteacher or management team of my school*

*delete as appropriate

What I like best about the way we work together in class/school is:

Something I'd like to change or develop in our work is:

Because:

Something I'd like (us) to learn more about is:

Because:

The way I'd like to learn about it is:

What I'm prepared to do about it is:

Communication

COMMUNICATION

MEMO RESPONSE ACTIVITY F

Individually/in pairs:
Read/discuss the memos you have and make some notes about their implications.

In pairs and then as a small group:
Discuss your individual reactions to the memos and think of some responses or strategies that might be appropriate.

Be ready to share your ideas with the others in the group.

MEMO TO THE CLASS TEACHER(S):

Something I'd like to change about my work is to get some more support from you and be included in the main lessons. When the lesson begins I am asked to work outside the classroom with the child.

Because you say that the child disrupts the lesson because he doesn't understand the work, so therefore I have to prepare separate work for him to do. He is in a mainstream school, so he should be included with the rest of the class.

Something I'd like to learn more about is his disability.

Because I have never had any dealings with this before.

The way I'd like to learn about it is in school with his teachers, so we will all have the same understanding.

What I enjoy most about my work is when the teacher is satisfied with my work, and the children enjoyed my assistance.

Communication

MEMO TO THE CLASS TEACHER(S):

Something I'd like to change about my work is to have time to communicate with each of you, e.g. on the subject of the lesson; what you want me to do during the lesson; time to tell you how the students have performed; the level of support given.

Because I would then know whether I am doing my job correctly; if not, where can I improve my performance, e.g. did your lesson go as planned with me in your classroom? If not, how can we improve?

Something I'd like to learn more about is the planning of lessons.

Because I would like to prepare myself for the subject being taught.

What I like best about my work is the rewards of working with the students.

Help in the Classroom

MEMO TO THE HEADTEACHER/ SENIOR MANAGEMENT TEAM

Something I'd like to change about my work is to have a written job description that I and other members of staff may relate to.

Because at the moment I feel as if I am floating from one job to another. If my own child does not need me, I sit in the classroom and help anyone who needs help. This *can* be beneficial, but quite often can be several hours of trying to settle disruptive children.

Something I'd like to learn more about is how to settle disruptive children. The skill to hold a child's attention and to gain his interest is very difficult, many teachers don't even manage this.

The way I'd like to learn is to take a course on social behaviour among children ... (details) ... and should we as assistants think we have the right or experience to delve too deeply?

What I like best about my work is seeing my one-to-one child develop and grow and do things I never thought we would see six years ago.

MEMO TO THE HEADTEACHER/ SENIOR MANAGEMENT TEAM

Something I'd like to change about my work is the attitude of some teachers to my presence in class, plus the lack of information about the planned lessons.

Because going in blind to some lessons is very disconcerting and disorientating and hampers my ability to help the students who need it.

Something I'd like to learn more about is IT, as it is becoming a more important part of education.

Because at present I am way out of my depth with regard to it and am unable to be much, if any, help.

The way I'd like to learn about it is on an out-of-school course, because there will be no way that you can be distracted by being called away for a work-related reason.

What I like best about my work is the sense of achievement when you have helped a student to understand and do a task they were thought of as never being able to grasp or understand.

CONSISTENCY OF APPROACH

Learning support assistants should be seen positively as part of the range of provision to meet children's and students' educational needs

AIM
To examine how two adults, sharing a classroom in order to meet the needs of the children, can work most effectively.

DOGSBODY

Cameo: An assistant describes her anxieties about something planned for the next half term:

> I'm going to support in Mrs M's class after half term because some of the children have moved on. She's never worked with anybody in the classroom before. She stuck out to be left out of the team teaching that was set up last year. It's a shame these children I need to work with are in *her* class, but they do need some support. I hope it'll be all right!

ACTIVITY
Sharing classrooms

Individually:

- Consider the situation described by the assistant.
- Think of all the potential difficulties arising:
    - for Mrs M
    - for the assistant
    - for the children.

As a group:
1. Share your ideas about the problems you foresee for Mrs M, the assistant, the children.
2. List them on a flipchart.
3. Attempt to identify the problems which could be generalised to other situations when two adults are sharing a classroom.
4. Mark them (e.g. with a star) on the list.
5. Think of the things you are planning to do in the school in the next few weeks/next term that you feel might be made more successful by having considered the issues you have marked.
6. Attempt to draw up a set of ground rules that you would find useful for:
    - the teacher(s)
    - the assistant(s)
    - the children.

As whole group:
Share these ground rules if you have been working in more than one group and agree a composite list for the whole group.

Coordinator:
- Refer here to the guidance on working out an action plan at level 1 or moving to level 2.

Now draw up your action plan.

When doing this think about:

- How to implement your ground rules.
- Which are the most important?
- Which could you do reasonably easily and swiftly?
- Are there some you could try out in working pairs?

Use your outline sheet as individuals to contribute to the whole group plan.

Consistency of Approach　　　　　　　　　　　　　　　　　　　　　　　　**65**

CONSISTENCY OF APPROACH

Learning support assistants should be seen positively as part of the range of provision to meet children's and students' educational needs

AIM
To encourage staff to see learning support assistants as a positive resource that should be used consistently to meet children's needs.

DOGSBODY

Cameo:
A teacher:

> It doesn't matter if they have their break in the secretary's office, the staffroom's too small as it is for all the teachers.

An assistant:

> The atmosphere in the staffroom can be difficult, it depends on which teachers are there. Some would probably prefer us not to be there, others welcome us as 'one of the staff'.

BRICK WALLS

ACTIVITY

Individually:
1. Consider what is getting in the way of consistency of approaches in the above situation.
2. Has it, or something similar, happened in your school?
3. Using the Brick Wall outline think of all the things in your school that get in the way of achieving the objective behind the wall.
4. Fill these in (simply – a word or a phrase) on the blank bricks on your wall. These represent 'blocks' – what gets in the way. Do it *without* discussing it.
NB It is not necessary to fill in *every* block!

As a group:
1. On a large/flipchart Brick Wall blank build up a group Brick Wall by taking a block from each member of the group in turn. If more than one person has the same 'block' put a mark in the brick (each time it is duplicated).
2. Discuss the blocks using the following questions to guide you:
   (a) Are there any blocks that we can remove immediately by taking some action:
   as individuals (teachers/assistants)?
   together as a team?
   Mark these with a green tick.
   (b) Are there any blocks we feel we can do nothing about – they are 'beyond our control' – at least for the present? (So let's not worry about what we can do nothing about!)
   Mark these with a red cross.
   (c) Are there any blocks we feel we could work at removing over a period of time:
   as individuals (teachers/assistants)?
   together as a team?
   Mark these with a green question mark.

Now draw up your action plan.

You have already identified priorities for the short term action(s) and longer term ones.

When drawing up the action plan, build these in.

Individuals may like to return to their individual walls and check to see if there is some personal action they can take, as well as what is agreed on the group action plan.

Objective: Learning support assistants should be seen positively as part of the range of provision to meet children's and students' needs

Consistency of Approach

CONSISTENCY OF APPROACH

Classroom strategies activity

AIM
To explore in detail classroom strategies and approaches, with some suggestions on a stimulus grid to initiate discussion. These are real examples offered by assistants in describing their classroom work, and focus on inclusive practices in primary schools. The discussion then encourages the sharing of ideas and practice amongst teachers and assistants. A consideration of a wide range of management strategies, focusing on the activities of assistants in supporting inclusive classroom practices, then leads to the opportunity to plan some development in classroom partnerships and collaboration.

ACTIVITY
Individually:
1. Read the suggestions offered on the grid – you will see that they all describe the assistant's activities.
2. Tick any that you have personally experienced, as teachers or assistants.
3. In the blank boxes add any additional strategies that you have personally found helpful as you have worked with another adult and which have had positive outcomes for you and the children.
4. Mark with a star the two most effective ideas, either those already offered or your own additions.

In pairs:
Discuss what you have each experienced and any additions you have made.

Tell each other why you found these strategies positive and how they came about. In particular focus on the two starred ones.

In small groups:
1. Each person in turn tell the others about the chosen two strategies.
2. As a group decide on one that you think is particularly important in encouraging inclusive practice.
3. Draw up an outline plan of how it would be prepared and put into practice in a typical classroom (include staff development needs) and then reviewed and evaluated, with indicators of successful implementation stated clearly.

Whole group:
1. Debrief the activity with each group in turn describing their chosen strategy and their plans for using it in practice.
2. Collect all these plans together to be collated and distributed among participants.
3. Agree a date when you will meet again to see how you have all got on with trying out a strategy in practice.

Individually:
Reflect on what you have learnt about strategies which support inclusive learning through effective collaboration in the classroom.

Think how you personally might use the ideas discussed.

CLASSROOM STRATEGIES

	Learning support assistant has overall curriculum plan in advance – so is able to respond, prepare, work as appropriate.	Learning support assistant feels that she/he has adequate 'skill-area' preparation for the task in hand, e.g. literacy strategies, observation approaches.
	Learning support assistant is encouraged, through flexible teaching and learning styles, to engage fully when necessary, stand back as appropriate.	
Learning support assistant has a range of strategies learnt at a staff development session, for encouraging 'on-task' behaviour.		Learning support assistant feels she/he can offer feedback to the teacher after the lesson about how it went, her/his part in it, children's activities etc.
Notes:		

CONSISTENCY OF APPROACH

CLASSROOM STRATEGIES ACTIVITY – DEVELOPING GUIDANCE

AIM
To develop discussions about classroom strategies which support inclusive learning, through the effective collaboration of teachers and assistants. The activity is aimed at providing staff development and training for teachers in managing assistants in their classrooms. The focus in this activity is the management strategies that teachers use and can develop in their classroom practice with assistants. The grid provides some examples given by assistants in their analysis of how teachers have used positive management strategies with them in primary school classrooms.

ACTIVITY
Individually:
1. Read the suggestions offered on the grid – you will see that they all describe the teacher's management strategies.
2. Tick any that you have personally experienced, as teachers or assistants.
3. In the blank boxes add any additional strategies that you have personally found helpful as you have worked with another adult and which have had positive outcomes for you and the children.

In pairs/small groups:
1. Tell each other what you have written and why.
2. Create a composite list of all the strategies that as a group you have added to the ones offered on the grid, and any amendments to those.
3. Write them down on a flipchart sheet and post them on the wall.

Whole group:
1. Consider each of the group lists in turn with group members answering questions or elaborating on them.
2. Use these to create a master list for distribution throughout the staff team as guidelines for developing practice.

Individually;
Reflect on your own learning. Has there been an idea that you and a colleague could work on and develop in your partnership in the classroom? When might you do it and how?

CLASSROOM STRATEGIES –
DEVELOPING GUIDANCE

	Teacher has clarified issues of discipline – levels of intervention expected from the assistant – with both assistant and children.	Teacher has encouraged assistant to stand back from time to time so that children work more independently.
Teacher planned the lesson with assistant's presence in mind, in particular with reference to approaches with one child/small group(s) of children.		Teacher has differentiated a set of materials with certain children in mind and prepared these for the assistant/asked the assistant to modify them.
	Teacher has set an ethos of professional regard for the assistant which children pick up on – both expecting and giving feedback on lesson outcomes.	
Notes:		

Consistency of Approach

CONSISTENCY OF APPROACH

CLASSROOM STRATEGIES ACTIVITY

AIM

To explore in detail classroom strategies and approaches, with some suggestions on a stimulus grid to initiate discussion. These are real examples offered by assistants in describing their classroom work, and focus on inclusive practices in secondary schools. The discussion then encourages the sharing of ideas and practice among teachers and assistants. A consideration of a wide range of management strategies, focusing on the activities of assistants in supporting inclusive classroom practices, then leads to the opportunity to plan some development in classroom partnerships and collaboration.

Individually:
1. Read the suggestions offered on the grid – you will see that they all describe the assistant's activities.
2. Tick any that you have personally experienced, as teachers or assistants.
3. In the blank boxes add any additional strategies that you have personally found helpful as you have worked with another adult and which have had positive outcomes for you and the students.
4. Mark with a star the two most effective ideas, either those already offered or your own additions.

In pairs:
Discuss what you have each experienced and any additions you have made.
Tell each other why you found these strategies positive and how they came about.
In particular focus on the two starred ones.

In small groups:
1. Each person in turn tells the others about the chosen two strategies.
2. As a group decide on one that you think is particularly important in encouraging inclusive practice.
3. Draw up an outline plan of how it would be prepared and put into practice in a typical classroom (include staff development needs, any discussions required with students, any liaison through subject groups) and then reviewed and evaluated, with indicators of successful implementation stated clearly.

Whole group:
1. Debrief the activity with each group in turn describing their chosen strategy and their plans for using it in practice.
2. Collect all these plans together to be collated and distributed amongst participants.
3. Agree a date when you will meet again to see how you have all got on with trying out at least one strategy in practice.

Individually:
Reflect on what you have learnt about strategies which support inclusive learning through effective collaboration in the classroom.

Think how you personally might use the ideas discussed.

CLASSROOM STRATEGIES

	Learning support assistant is in possession before the lesson of the content/aims of the lesson, and its specific place in the overall curriculum/module.	Learning support assistant observes small group of mixed ability students working on collaborative task – focus: individual group members' contributions and achievements (using preprepared schedule).
Learning support assistant has been in discussion in advance with teacher(s) *and* students negotiating levels of support needed and independence possible.	Learning support assistant is able to work flexibly at different stages of the lesson as teaching and learning styles in progress are not overly formal.	
Learning support assistant works with several groups of students, each containing a 'difficult character', (*not* all of these in one group for the whole lesson).		Learning support assistant feels welcomed positively into the lesson by the teacher, so setting the tone – a cue for the students to follow.
Notes:		

Consistency of Approach

CONSISTENCY OF APPROACH

CLASSROOM STRATEGIES ACTIVITY – DEVELOPING GUIDANCE

AIM
To develop discussions about classroom strategies which support inclusive learning, through the effective collaboration of teachers and assistants. The activity is aimed at providing staff development and training for teachers in managing assistants in their classroom. The focus in this activity is the management strategies that teachers use and can develop in their classroom practice with assistants. The grid provides some examples given by assistants in their analysis of how teachers have used positive management strategies with them in secondary schools.

ACTIVITY
Individually:
1. Read the suggestions offered on the grid – you will see that they all describe the teacher's management strategies.
2. Tick any that you have personally experienced, as teachers or assistants.
3. In the blank boxes add any additional strategies that you have personally found helpful as you have worked with another adult and which have had positive outcomes for you and the students. Indicate examples where this was subject specific.

In pairs/small groups:
1. Tell each other what you have written and why.
2. Create a composite list of all the strategies that as a group you have added to the ones offered on the grid, and any amendments to those.
3. Write them down on a flipchart sheet and post them on the wall.

Whole group:
1. Consider each of the group lists in turn with group members answering questions or elaborating on them.
2. Use these to create a master list for distribution throughout the staff team as guidelines for developing practice.

Individually:
Reflect on your own learning. Has there been an idea that you and a colleague could work on and develop in your partnership in the classroom? When might you do it and how?

Help in the Classroom

CLASSROOM STRATEGIES – DEVELOPING GUIDANCE

	Teacher has clarified issues of discipline – levels of intervention expected from the learning support assistant (with assistant *and* students).	
Teacher(s) planned the lesson with assistant's presence in mind, in particular with reference to approaches with one student/small group(s) of students.	Teacher has encouraged assistant to 'stand back' from time to time – so student(s) work independently (and perhaps to make observation notes) or work as resource to any student.	Teacher has differentiated a set of materials with certain students in mind and prepared these for the assistant/asked the assistant to modify them.
	Teacher has set an ethos of professional regard for the assistant which students 'pick up on' – taking a lead from the learning support coordinator.	Teacher has given the assistant a small card of 'do's and don'ts' re complex areas related to, materials, equipment, skills and safety (especially in 'technical' curricular area)
Notes:		

CONSISTENCY OF APPROACH

The place of professional relationships

AIM

To consider how consistency of approaches to the work of assistants in classrooms often hinges on the relationships formed between those working together. This activity explores the nature of professional relationships that assistants experience and would also like to develop with teaching and other colleagues, the children and students, their parents and others who work in and visit the school.

Individually:

Note down all the relationships you experience during the course of a week at school.
List them under the following headings:

Regular   *Occasional*

Concentrating on the Regular column first, consider:

- Which are the relationships you feel to be 'professional'?
- Why? What makes them feel so?
- Which are the difficult ones?
- Why? Where do the difficulties lie?

Then consider the Occasional column in the same way.

In pairs:

Share what you have written down.

Consider the following:

The 'professional' relationships – what are their characteristics?

The difficult ones – why do they feel like this?

How can you use the positive experiences to help provide guidance on the difficult ones?

Be ready to share the main points with the whole group.

Whole group:

Explore the issues that have been raised.

Generate and record positive features and strategies which assist the development of positive and professional relationships.

Individually:

Reflect on your own situation and the notes you made.
Complete the '**Ideas for Action**' sheet.
Share these with your original partner.

Help in the Classroom

CONSISTENCY OF APPROACH

The place of professional relationships

IDEAS FOR ACTION SHEET

Ideas for action   **Date:**

I will:

I would like to:

The small team/we could or should:

The school team as a whole should:

My (one!) wish would be:

Action points

The relationship I will focus on:

What I will do:

When (date/time/opportunity):

What I will say:

When (date/time/opportunity):

What I hope will happen as a result:

Who I may need to seek support from:

Review notes   **Date:**

In discussion with:

A WORKING TEAM

Learning support assistants should be members of a working team

AIM

To consider how many assistants may be involved as members of a working team, through information sharing and problem solving. In this context every member's contribution is valued as having inherent worth.

A SPY IN THE CLASSROOM

Cameo: An assistant's observation:

> I think if some teachers were 100 per cent honest they would admit that they think of us as 'second class citizens', and they just can't see the potential we have to offer as part of the team.

ACTIVITY

'Tom'

Bearing in mind the above comment, and with the idea of information sharing and problem solving, you will now be considering the story of 'Tom'. This activity will help you think about the team's information sharing and problem solving strategies.

As a small group:

- Share one set of the cards out evenly among the group(s), randomly, face down.
- Do not allow anyone to see what is written on the cards you are dealt.
- Share the information on the cards verbally.
- Do not:
    show them to each other,
    put them in the middle of the group, or
    write down on a corporate list.
- You may make notes for your own personal use.

On the cards you each have a range of information, some of which is useful, some of which are red herrings.

As a group you need to pool the information and come to some decisions about course(s) of action which might be taken given the situation presented to you. The question is: 'What should the school and the individuals be doing about Tom?'

After detailed discussion, and having made some decisions about possible courses of action, debrief the activity (either in small groups or in the larger group).

In small group:
1. Briefly describe the course of action your group decided and why that was so.
2. Spend more time on considering what you learnt from the process you went through of information sharing and problem solving:

- what you learnt individually?
- what you contributed individually?
- what you learnt as a group?

As a whole group:
Consider your courses of action with regard to sharing information and developing team problem solving. Base your decision making for action on the issues you have been considering and how every member of the team could be part of the plan of action for you as a team.

Coordinator: refer here to the guidance on working out an action plan at level 1 or moving to level 2.

Help in the Classroom

TOM

(Note. Boxes should be enlarged and cut up as single slips of paper/card for dissemination around the group)

Miss Sterne is very insistent on children arriving in time for school

Tom has difficulty getting up in the morning

Tom's older sister experienced a lot of problems in school

Tom Atkinson is eleven

On the school's reading assessment Tom has a reading age of 6.5

Tom's artwork is outstanding

At home Tom spends a lot of time playing computer games

Mrs Jones reports that Tom has been very difficult in her groups

Mrs Atkinson gets very lonely during the day

Tom's best friend George is in a year group two years below him

Tom goes to Scouts on Tuesday evenings

Tom dislikes lessons where the teacher does a lot of talking to the class

Sometimes Tom gets sent to Miss Sterne for misbehaving

Tom misses out on rewards like the computer or robot games

Tom's concentration on written tasks is very poor

Jenny says Tom hit her twice yesterday

Tom has great difficulty in following class instructions

The extra reading help that he has received for the last three years does not seem to have worked with Tom

Tom's Grandad has just bought him a Subbuteo game

Mrs Jenkins, the assistant, enjoys doing art with the children

Tom loves his dog

Recently Tom's dog has been ill

Mrs Jones takes Tom for extra reading three times a week

Tom's father died when he was two years old

Mrs Atkinson sometimes works on a night shift in a factory

Tom is a keen Liverpool fan

Mr Roberts, Tom's maths teacher, insists on silence in the class during most of the lesson

Tom is very overweight

Tom's teacher believes in rigorous P.E. lessons

Tom is not popular with most of the other children in the year group

A WORKING TEAM

Learning support assistants should be members of a working team

AIM
To examine the staff's development with regard to including the assistants in an effective working team, at whole-school level.

A SPY IN THE CLASSROOM

Cameo: An assistant:

> I'm not sure that if we each tried to explain what we're trying to do as a team the explanations and reasons would be the same. People assume... but you find it's not always as open as you think.

ACTIVITY
Memo Exercise
To allow some consideration of the above issues in a non-threatening way anonymous memos will be written and then examined by everybody as a group. Clarification and discussion should result in some understanding and openness about the issues raised.

Individually:
Group members fill in the Memo Exercise sheet they have been given.

These should be placed in a box.

As a group:
1. Each person in the group picks out a Memo sheet, reads it to the group and makes a comment in response to set the ball rolling. If someone picks out their own, they should put it back and take another.
2. Discuss each of the Memos in turn. Consider the implications of each of the statements – are they raising previously unknown difficulties or issues for people? Is there anything that suggests immediate action that:

   - one person could take?
   - a group of people could take?
   - the whole school might work on?

Now draw up an action plan.

MEMO EXERCISE

Complete the following sentence with three (maximum) suggestions.

Think of the things *you* would like to do to contribute.

Think of the things you think other people either ought to do, or perhaps could think about.

Think about the team as a whole – what would you like it to do?

In order for our team to work well, I would like:

-

-

-

Help in the Classroom

A WORKING TEAM

Partnerships in the classroom

AIM

To explore the development of a working team that starts in classroom partnerships. These partnerships might be termed 'learning partnerships'. They foster staff development in classroom contexts and what is learnt within them may often be shared with colleagues in the wider team of the primary school. This activity offers the opportunity to consider the features that exist in successful learning partnerships, using the personal experiences of the staff in the school as a starting point and drawing on this to develop further ideas.

ACTIVITY

Individually:

- Think about your most significant classroom partnership.
- Write some notes about what you have learnt under the suggested headings for example:

    from my partner
    about our classroom practice
    about working with my partner
    about learning together in a partnership.

In pairs:

With someone who is not your regular partner in the classroom consider the learning you feel your partner and you have achieved about your work itself, and about the processes of working together.

Two significant features of effective learning partnership processes are those of *support* and *challenge* and the balance that exists between them.

You will find it helpful at this point to consider the outline reference sheet explaining the kinds of support and challenge that have been found to be helpful to learning partnerships by other practitioners in schools. With this in mind here are some questions for you to think about:

- What kinds of support do you and your partner gain from each other?
- How do you challenge each other's thinking in positive and constructive ways?
- How does this fit in with the traditional manager/managed relationship existing between teachers and assistants?

Individually:

1. Reflect on what you have learnt about your partnership work.
2. Complete the section asking you to consider what you already do and what else you and your partner(s) might also think of doing.

A WORKING TEAM

Partnerships in the classroom

Individually:

Think of your most significant classroom partnership, either with someone you spend most time together with in a classroom, or one that you particularly value from a range that you experience. Make some notes about what you have learnt with and from your partner about:

Classroom practice

Working together

Learning together

In pairs:

Discuss what you have each written, focusing on what you have learnt about the processes of working together:

How do you think you each support your partner?

In what ways do you challenge or question your partner, for example, their assumptions or strategies?

Individually:

Write down under the two headings of

	Support	Challenge

What I already do

What my partner does

What we might think of doing as well

Also, think whether any other of your classroom partnerships might benefit from more attention to the balance of support and challenge in order to experience positive learning outcomes.

A WORKING TEAM

Learning in classroom partnerships

AIM
To consider what has been learnt in and about classroom partnerships between teachers and assistants in the school; the balance that exists within them of challenge and support and the ways in which what has been learnt could be positively built on throughout the school. This is done through an activity that explores ideas already considered in pairs and small groups, builds on this process and seeks to offer guidance about learning in partnership that might be supportive of team development throughout the school.

Individually:
- Reflect on your most significant or frequent classroom partnership with a teacher or an assistant.
- Consider the outline notes on partnership learning and the notes you made on the 'Partnerships in the classroom' sheet.
- Think whether the aspects of support and challenge you outlined there have helped your learning in that or any other partnership since then.

In small groups:
1. Share your ideas about forms of support and challenge in your personal experiences of working in a partnership of teacher and assistant.
2. On a flipchart sheet, list all the examples you have of support experienced by group members.
3. Add all the examples of challenges experienced.
4. Mark with a tick any of these that you think helped your learning.
5. Put together some advice through finishing the following sentences:

   Assistants and teachers will develop more effective learning in partnerships if the following forms of *support* exist . . .

   Assistants and teachers will develop more effective learning in partnerships if the following forms of *challenge* exist . . .

6. Put these onto a new flipchart sheet and post it on the wall where others can see it.

Whole group:
Consider the advice posted from all the groups on the flipchart sheets.
Discuss which seem to be the key elements to draw from all the advice offered.
Compile a whole-group set of guidance on an OHP or flipchart about the conditions that will support partnership learning between teachers and assistants in the school in the future.
Make sure this is circulated to all participants later.

Individually:
Reflect on what you have learnt about partnership processes between assistants and teachers.

Consider:
- How will you personally encourage the partnership(s) in which you are involved to become (a) more productive learning partnership(s)?
- How will you see that this benefits the children you work with?
- What messages will they pick up from your working relationship and learning?

A WORKING TEAM

Partnerships in the classroom – some background notes on developing effective learning within classroom partnerships

Learning partnerships in classrooms are more likely to be effective if they offer forms of support and challenge to each partner. Learning itself means that individuals have to take risks. They are more likely to take these risks if they have someone at their side to learn with them. A teacher and an LSA are in an ideal position to form a learning partnership as they have to be together as part of the provision to meet children's and student's needs. Two people in a partnership will benefit from two key elements. These key elements have been identified by practitioners who have formed effective learning partnerships, particularly as they inquire into their classroom practices. They are *support* and *challenge*. The challenge provides forms of motivation and interest, while support helps the two partners to provide forms of moral, theoretical and practical help to one another. In addition there is a recognition that whether they are a teacher or an assistant they can each learn from the other as well as together.

Support means that:

- partners actively listen to each other;
- partners share ideas and concerns;
- partners are reflective together;
- partners relate to each other's contexts and situations.

Challenge means that:

- partners inquire further into ideas and opinions expressed;
- partners explore together strategies for problem solving;
- partners establish priorities for courses of action and their review;
- partners develop the capacity to be constructively critical;
- partners build accountability to each other into their plans.

All of this is helped through the negotiation of ground rules by the partners.

A WORKING TEAM

Partnerships in the classroom

AIM
To explore the development of a working team that starts in classroom partnerships. These partnerships might be termed 'learning partnerships'. They foster staff development in classroom contexts and what is learnt within them may often be shared with colleagues in the wider team of the secondary school. This activity offers the opportunity to consider the features that exist in successful learning partnerships, using the personal experiences of the staff in the school as a starting point and drawing on this to develop further ideas.

Individually:
Think about your most significant classroom partnership.

Write some notes about what you have learnt under the suggested headings, for example:

> from my partner
> about our classroom practice
> about working with my partner
> about learning together in a partnership.

In pairs:
With someone who is not your regular partner in the classroom consider the learning you feel your partner and you have achieved about your work itself, and about the processes of working together.

Two significant features of effective learning partnership processes are those of *support* and *challenge* and the balance that exists between them.

You will find it helpful at this point to consider the outline reference sheet explaining the kinds of support and challenge that have been found to be helpful to learning partnerships by other practitioners in schools. With this in mind, here are some questions for you to think about:

- What kinds of support do you and your partner gain from each other?
- How do you challenge each other's thinking in positive and constructive ways?
- How does this fit in with the traditional manager/managed relationship existing between teachers and assistants?

Individually:
1. Reflect on what you have learnt about your partnership work.
2. Complete the section asking you to consider what you already do and what else you and your partner(s) might also think of doing.

A Working Team

A WORKING TEAM

Partnerships in the classroom

Individually:

Think of your most significant classroom partnership, either with someone whom you spend some time together within a classroom or curriculum area, or one that you particularly value from a range that you experience. Make some notes about what you have learnt with and from your partner about:

Classroom practice

Working together

Learning together

In pairs:

Discuss what you have each written. Focusing on what you have learnt about the processes of working together:

How do you think you each support your partner?

In what ways do you challenge or question your partner, for example, their assumptions or strategies?

Individually:

Write down under the two headings of

	Support	*Challenge*
What I already do		
What my partner does		
What we might think of doing as well		

Also, think whether any other of your classroom partnerships might benefit from more attention to the balance of support and challenge in order to experience positive learning outcomes.

A WORKING TEAM

Learning in classroom partnerships

AIM

To consider what has been learnt in and about classroom partnerships between teachers and assistants in the school; the balance that exists within them of challenge and support and the ways in which what has been learnt could be positively built on throughout the school. This is done through an activity that explores ideas already considered in pairs and small groups, builds on this process and seeks to offer guidance about learning in partnership that might be supportive of team development throughout the school.

Individually:

- Reflect on your most significant or frequent classroom partnership with a teacher or an assistant.
- Consider the outline notes on partnership learning and the notes you made on the 'Partnerships in the classroom' sheet.
- Think whether the aspects of support and challenge you outlined there have helped your learning in that or any other partnership since then.

In small groups:

1. Share your ideas about forms of support and challenge in your personal experiences of working in a partnership of teacher and assistant.
2. On a flipchart sheet list all the examples you have of support experienced by group members.
3. Add all the examples of challenges experienced.
4. Mark with a tick any of these that you think helped your learning.
5. Put together some advice through finishing the following sentences:
   Assistants and teachers will develop more effective learning in partnerships if the following forms of *support* exist . . .

   Assistants and teachers will develop more effective learning in partnerships if the following forms of *challenge* exist . . .

6. Put these onto a new flipchart sheet and post it on the wall where others can see it.

Whole group:

Consider the advice posted from all the groups on the flipchart sheets.
Discuss which seem to be the key elements to draw from all the advice offered.
Compile a whole-group set of guidance on an OHP or flipchart about the conditions that will support partnership learning between teachers and assistants in the school in the future.
Make sure this is circulated to all participants later.

Individually:

Reflect on what you have learnt about partnership processes between assistants and teachers.

Consider:

- How will you personally encourage the partnership(s) in which you are involved to become (a) more productive learning partnership(s)?
- How will you see that this benefits the students with whom you work?
- What messages will they pick up from your working relationship and learning?

A WORKING TEAM

AIM

To consider the ways in which classroom partnerships may be developed and supported using assistants' own individual experiences of classroom situations. The activity leads to some action points that assistants identify which may support the development of their classroom collaboration and teamwork with teachers.

Individually:

Think of a recent lesson when you shared a classroom with a teacher.

Note down what you and the teacher did at different stages of the lesson.

Teacher	*Assistant*

In pairs:

Discuss what you each have on your lists.

In small groups:

Compare notes about the assistant's tasks/activities.

Ask yourselves the following questions:

- How prepared were you for the lesson?
- What were the aims for your tasks/the children's work?
- What kind of feedback did you give/get from the teacher and when?
- What do you feel the teacher and you learnt from each other?

Be ready to tell the others the main points of your discussions.

Whole group:

1. Each small group offer feedback on the four questions above.
2. Draw out some general principles that lead to the successful sharing of classrooms and team development, recording these on a flipchart.

Individually:

Reflect on the discussion and its implications for the next lesson like the one you described above – what have you learnt?

Write one or more action points to support some development in your immediate team's practice over which *you* have some control

---

Help in the Classroom

DEVELOPING PERSONAL SKILLS

Learning support assistants should be encouraged to make use of their personal and professional skills

OVERGROWN PUPIL

AIM
To consider how best the skills of everybody in the working team can be used with regard to a particular area of the curriculum. To unpack the skills, talents, likes and dislikes of the team members.

OVERGROWN PUPIL
Cameo: Some comments that assistants have made:

All this observation that has to be done for the National Curriculum, I could help with a lot more of that...

I worked on the National Trust's group that helped to restore that section of the canal...

I know it's a long time since I got my swimming certificate, but...

I did GCSE level French at night class in 1985...

ACTIVITY
Curriculum review

In twos and threes:
Consider a recent piece of work carried out by a teacher(s) and assistant(s) in the classroom, on a curriculum area (e.g. a series of maths lessons), some cross-curricular topic work, or a one-off activity, bearing in mind some of the above comments.

Some questions to help your thinking:
- How well did it work?
- How was each of the adults' skills and knowledge utilised?
- Were all the skills you could each have used put to good effect?

Make some statements:
- With hindsight I...
- With hindsight we...

As a whole group:
Generate a set of questions or guidelines you could run through to guide yourselves, using the benefit of hindsight, in your next piece(s) of curriculum planning.

Put these onto the flipchart.

Coordinator:
Refer here to the guidance on working out an action plan at level 1 or moving to level 2.

Now draw up your action plan, to put these questions/guidelines into effect within your working team(s).

Decide which particular piece of the curriculum you will plan for and make that the short term objective so you have a clear focus.

Developing Personal Skills

DEVELOPING PERSONAL SKILLS

Learning support assistants should be encouraged to make use of their personal and professional skills

AIM

To create an atmosphere in which people are able to explore their contributions to the learning environment of the school, in ways that will facilitate the progress of all pupils.

Cameo:
A teacher about an assistant:

> She's just an assistant, she shouldn't be asked to help with planning the topic work we're going to cover in science and humanities.

The assistant thinks:

> But I haven't had the chance to tell her about the work I've done with the nature conservancy organisation – that would be very useful for this topic.

ACTIVITY: A Visitor exercise

This activity allows each member of the group to have the 'platform'.

Considering the above scenario, and the perceived waste of talent and dismissive nature of the teacher's comment, this activity seeks to help you as a team to examine the skills, talents, likes, dislikes etc. of your team members, and then to capitalise on them.

Coordinator: If you have a group of two, it is helpful to enlist at least one extra person to be involved in this exercise, either within the discussion or as an observer to debrief.

Larger groups may also choose to have an observer and there is an observation schedule attached which you can use to debrief the group process.

Group activity:
The chosen (or volunteer) visitor leaves the room and the rest of the group prepare to receive this visitor into the group as a guest. The observer watches this and what follows when the visitor arrives.

The group has to decide on how to:
- put the visitor at ease;
- elicit as much information as possible without appearing to 'grill' the visitor;
- agree which roles they will each perform and the questions they will put.

The following list helps the discussion:
- likes and dislikes about the job
- personal opinions, preferences, etc.
- hopes and fears about the job
- interests outside school
- unfulfilled wishes (you might have a once hopeful Olympic swimmer in your midst!)
- something which might help improve working life.

This discussion should take *no longer* than ten minutes and less if there is only a pair to discuss with the visitor.

Invite the visitor in and conduct your activity as you have planned it.

Debrief:
- How did the visitor feel?
- How did the rest of the group feel?
- What did the observer see?
- What have you learnt about individuals in the team?

Now draw up your action plan

Bearing in mind curriculum planning at present being undertaken in the school/team/department: how do you now feel you can best use the skills and talents of both assistants and teachers in the future?

Use some of the key areas (objectives) each person has described which might for them as individuals, and for the team, improve:
- practice in the classroom
- job satisfaction
- identification of good practice which can be built on.

Help in the Classroom

OBSERVATION SCHEDULE

DECISION MAKING PERIOD
How were the decisions reached about how the session should go?

Who took the lead?

VISITOR IN THE GROUP
How comfortable did the visitor appear to be?
- initially?

- throughout the session?

In what ways did the group members elicit the information they sought?

How much did they encourage dialogue rather than 'interrogation'?

How well did they appear to achieve their objectives?

Further comments (objective) about approaches to the task, e.g. listening, encouraging.

DEVELOPING PERSONAL AND PROFESSIONAL SKILLS

AIM

To explore the skills of individuals in the school at coordinating the work with assistants and developing learning in partnerships. This will be done through the use of a schedule focused on developing knowledge and those skills necessary to fulfil the role. In addition particular attention is paid to the work of assistants in the school. Potential staff development needs are a focus within this schedule and it supports the identification of appropriate responses within the primary school.

Individually:

Complete the schedule on the skills of the coordinator as suggested. Remember that:

- you are looking first at your current skills, i.e. what you feel confident and competent about, then at potential needs;
- you are also concentrating on the work of assistants in the school, from your own perspective and experience; for example, as a learning support coordinator you will have specific responsibilities in this area; as a class teacher with assistant support you will have classroom management responsibilities for that person; as an assistant you will be working in partnerships which necessitate the use of liaison and support skills;
- in particular, you should focus on the staff development needs identified through this process.

In pairs:

- Discuss what you have each written in response to each item.
- Work collaboratively to produce an individual action plan for each of you, following the suggestions made.
- Remember to identify forms of support and evaluation.

Whole group:

1. As pairs tell the others each of your main points of action.
2. As whole group draw up a list of actions, support, liaison etc. needed with and by people not in this discussion, but crucial to making things happen. Are there meeting agendas, for example, where some of these issues should be raised?

Individually:

Reflect on what you have written on your plan:

- what have you learnt about your own knowledge and skills in coordinating activities and people?
- what impact will the developments you have suggested have on your practice?

Help in the Classroom

USING PERSONAL AND PROFESSIONAL SKILLS

AIM
To explore the skills of individuals in the school at coordinating the work with assistants and developing learning in partnerships. This will be done through the use of a schedule focused on developing knowledge and those skills necessary to fulfil the role. In addition particular attention is paid to the work of assistants in the school. Potential staff development needs are a focus within this schedule and it supports the identification of appropriate responses, in the context of a secondary school.

Individually:
Complete the schedule on the skills of the coordinator as suggested. Remember that:
- you are looking first, at your current skills, i.e. what you feel confident and competent about, then potential needs;
- you are also concentrating on the work of assistants in the school, from your own perspective and experience; for example, as a learning support coordinator you will have specific responsibilities in this area; as a class teacher with assistant support you will have classroom management responsibilities for that person; as a curriculum leader your accountabilities may include developing practice and liaising with assistants who work in and with your department; as an assistant you will be working in partnerships which necessitate the use of liaison and support skills;
- in particular, you should focus on the staff development needs identified through this process.

In pairs:
- Discuss what you have each written in response to each item.
- Work collaboratively to produce an individual action plan for each of you, following the suggestions made.
- Remember to identify forms of support and evaluation.

Whole group:
1. As pairs tell the others each of your main points of action.
2. As whole group draw up a list of actions, support, liaison etc. needed with and by people not in this discussion, but crucial to making things happen. Are there meeting agendas, for example, where some of these issues should be raised? Should subject departments take some action? Is the senior management team or staff development coordinator implicated?

Individually:
Reflect on what you have written on your plan:
- what have you learnt about your own knowledge and skills in coordinating activities and people?
- what impact will the developments you have suggested have on your practice?

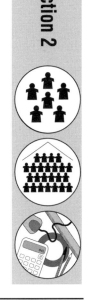

Developing Personal Skills

SKILLS OF THE COORDINATOR

Research suggests that the following skills seem to be important to success in coordinating groups of adults in the development of practice. Make some notes about your own skills in these areas:

1. Developing a clear purpose for activities

2. Establishing rapport with colleagues

3. Leading meetings and other group activities

4. Maintaining interest and enthusiasm

5. Resolving problems, including difficulties over relationships

6. Encouraging collaboration

7. Providing support

8. Keeping people informed

Source: *Creating the Conditions for School Improvement* (Ainscow *et al.* 1994b)

ACTION PLAN

In pairs:

When you have completed your notes form a partnership with a colleague. Discuss what you have been writing and why. Then go on to plan how you would assist one another in developing your skills as coordinators. Use each others' knowledge as a resource to support each plan.

Make some notes of actions that you plan to take to develop your skills as a coordinator.

1. My goals are...

2. To achieve these goals I intend to...

3. The problems I anticipate are...

4. I will seek support from...

Review date:

Developing Personal Skills

DEVELOPING PERSONAL AND PROFESSIONAL SKILLS

AIM
To explore practice in the school through a consideration of a set of review questions. The discussion focuses on the practice and skills which encourage teaching staff to explore with assistants what strengths they have to offer to the classroom environment and learning opportunities for children in a primary school.

Individually:
Consider the questions on the review of practice sheet.

Write a few notes about any of the questions that strike you as an individual to be important from your particular experiences and perspective.

In small groups:
Discuss the notes you have made in response to the questions. Are any of the concerns common to other members of the group?

Draw up a list of ideas about how you and others in the school might address these issues through staff development opportunities; for example, by raising agenda items in appropriate meetings, or developing partnership learning in the classroom.

Whole group:
Consider the issues raised and under the following headings list action points and those who might take action:

- assistants and teachers through partnership learning in the classroom;
- department or year teams at meetings;
- senior management, through policy development and organisation;
- staff development coordinator through the staff development plan, including both in-school opportunities and external courses.

Individually:
Reflect on:

- what you have learnt about the skills, knowledge and experience of assistants in the school;
- whether these are used to offer learning opportunities to children, assistants and teachers;
- how they might be developed further;
- what you can do personally to assist this process;
- what you might learn through doing this.

Help in the Classroom

REVIEW QUESTIONS

Do you know what skills, strengths and knowledge assistants can offer in the classroom?

Do you feel that assistants' skills and ideas have been utilised in order to support curriculum opportunities in the classroom?

In year groups or departments have you discussed the ways in which these skills can be capitalised on?

Is the management team aware of the skills and knowledge of assistants in the school?

Has a form of appraisal been carried out in support of this?

Have the staff development needs of assistants been considered within staff development planning?

Do they attend staff development sessions aimed at meeting their needs on a regular basis?

Do assistants' job descriptions and contracts reflect a proportion of staff development opportunities during paid hours?

Notes:

DEVELOPING PERSONAL AND PROFESSIONAL SKILLS

AIM

To explore practice in the school through a consideration of a set of review questions. The discussion focuses on the practice and skills which encourage teaching staff to explore with assistants what strengths they have to offer to the classroom environment and learning opportunities for students in a secondary school.

Individually:

Consider the questions on the review of practice sheet.

Write a few notes about any of the questions that strike you as an individual to be important from your particular experiences and perspective.

In small groups:

Discuss the notes you have made in response to the questions. Are any of the concerns common to other members of the group?

Draw up a list of ideas about how you and others in the school might address these issues: through staff development opportunities, raising agenda items in appropriate meetings; discussing them when planning at subject department level; or developing partnership learning in the classroom.

Whole group:

Consider the issues raised and under the following headings list action points and those who might take action:

- assistants and teachers through partnership learning in the classroom;
- subject department or year teams at meetings;
- senior management, through policy development and organisation;
- staff development coordinator through the staff development plan, including both in-school opportunities and external courses.

Individually:

Reflect on:

- what you have learnt about the skills, knowledge and experience of assistants in the school;
- whether these are used to offer learning opportunities to students, assistants and teachers;
- how they might be developed further;
- what you can do personally to assist this process;
- what you might learn through doing this.

REVIEW QUESTIONS

Do you know what skills, strengths and knowledge assistants can offer to particular classrooms and curriculum subjects?

Do you feel that assistants' skills and ideas have been utilised in order to support curriculum opportunities in the classroom?

In year groups or departments have you discussed the ways in which these skills can be capitalised on?

Is the management team aware of the skills and knowledge of assistants in the school?

Has a form of appraisal been carried out in support of this?

Are assistants allocated to appropriate curriculum areas, i.e. where they can play to their strengths, wherever possible during timetable planning?

Have the staff development needs of assistants been considered within staff development planning?

Do they attend staff development sessions aimed at meeting their needs on a regular basis?

Do assistants' job descriptions and contracts reflect a proportion of staff development opportunities during paid hours?

Notes:

Developing Personal Skills

DEVELOPING PERSONAL AND PROFESSIONAL SKILLS

AIM

To review the personal and professional strengths of assistants and to plan how these can be supported, while taking account of needs for futher development and taking measures to support weaknesses or prevent difficulties arising. A process of self-review and planning, in partnership with other assistants, assists this self-reflection.

Individually:

Complete the review of skills sheet.

Think carefully about the questions and answer them as honestly as you can – remember to be proud of what you can do and candid about things where you lack confidence.

Examples that might help to get you going might be: a good curriculum area or subject for you, or particularly good relationships/liaison with a teacher, child or parent. In contrast – what about something you dread doing or a classroom you have to pluck up courage to walk into? Think carefully of your own situation(s).

This review sheet is for your own eyes, but you will be asked to discuss it with one other assistant.

In pairs:

Go through each item on the sheet in turn together.

Think about:

- how positive and confident you feel about some aspects;
- how other people have enabled you to capitalise on your skills;
- how you feel about difficulties you face and whether they are due to your own lack of skills, or more to do with the way you are managed or how people relate to you (some of these difficulties may not be of your own making!); also
- what opportunities for support and the development of your learning you would like to see.

Whole group:

Focus on strengths and tell the rest of the group what your partner should feel confident about.

In pairs:

Use the action plan sheet to plan how to develop something you need some support with, training for example, or classroom based activities that will help you to gain confidence in working with a curriculum subject, a particular child or children, or a teacher.

Be ready to tell the rest of the group what you and your partner have planned.

Whole group:

Listen to everybody's plans, again each partner explaining *briefly* what the other person intends to do.

Agree a date when you will all meet again and review how you have got on.

Individually:

Reflect on what you are good at and feel pleased about.

Think of what you want to develop and how.

Does the difficulty/challenge already seem lessened by a positive plan?

REVIEW OF SKILLS

These are my strengths, skills, experiences:

I use them in the following situations:

I would like to use them . . .

Something I know I'm not confident about is . . .

To help me overcome, or if necessary, avoid this I would like . . .

ACTION PLAN

My focus/area of interest for development: **Date:**

Action points

I will . . .

I will do this/these by . . .

I will need support/commitment in school from . . .

They will need to . . .

Resources/time/practical materials that I will need are . . .

Possible obstacles might be . . .

Review with/on   **Partner:**   **Date:**

_____

Reflect on what has happened, what helped, what hindered and what is needed next.

STAFF DEVELOPMENT NEEDS

Learning support assistants should be supported in the development of their personal and professional skills

AIM

To identify staff development (INSET) needs, both in terms of the ways people like to learn, as well as what they want to learn. This includes a recognition that learning 'on the job' can be a very effective method of staff development.

LEFT UP IN THE AIR

Cameo:

A statement by an assistant:

> I went to my in-service course on Wednesday afternoons, and I don't normally work on Wednesday afternoons! I gave that up out of my own time to go on the course, and I think that in a way if you've taken time to do this it might be recognised somewhere along the line.

ACTIVITY

Card sorting

The aim of this activity is to attempt to avoid situations like the one given above. It does this by examining some forms of staff development and people's needs and preferences within these, and by helping the team to plan to meet these needs with particular reference to assistants.

Individually:

Each member of the group has a set of cards to sort into three piles. These are:

1. approaches to staff development/INSET which you have experienced;
2. approaches to staff development/INSET which you have not experienced;
3. approaches that need some explanation or you are not sure about.

Look again at 2. and sort these further into

    2(a)   have not experienced, but might like to try;
    2(b)   have not experienced and do not seem relevant to your work.

In pairs:

- Share/compare individual choices, seek clarification (then in fours if the group is big enough).
- Think of things experienced which you would like to try again.
- Think of ideas new to you (Pile 2a).
- Use the blank cards for any of your own ideas.
- Represent your own INSET ideas if they are not among the others.

As a group:

1. Enter into some identification and negotiation about people's needs, preferences and priorities.
2. Record these on a flipchart.
3. Identify courses of action for the following:
   - assistants
   - teachers
   - the team as a group
   - INSET coordinator/staff tutor
   - INSET providers.

Coordinator: refer here to the guidance on working out an action plan at level 1 or moving to level 2.

Now draw up your action plan.

Keep the following questions in mind:

- Are there any ideas which the team can plan and organise for itself?
- What skills are present within the group to assist this?
- What does the staff development coordinator for the school need to know about?
- How will you meet individual needs/team needs through the plan?
- How will you know you have met the needs?

(These boxes should be cut into individual cards)

In-service course outside school in working hours	Staff meeting/professional development meeting in school in working hours
Negotiations with regard to the content of the session(s) to be undertaken	In-service involving – discussion groups – workshop tasks – active involvement
In-service course counting for a (further) qualification	In-service involving – input e.g. lecture – skills based learning – demonstration
A course or series of sessions suggesting tasks to try in the classroom between sessions	Using self-assessment as a means of identifying requirements and starting points of the participant
Feedback session on ideas tried out in the classroom, evaluation of success	Using development of learning/curriculum materials as a form of staff development

Using problem solving as a form of staff development	Using case studies as a form of staff development
Using role-play as a form of staff development	Using simulation as a form of staff development
Staff development employing content related to your everyday work in the classroom	Staff development employing content related to an area of work you would like to develop

STAFF DEVELOPMENT NEEDS

Learning support assistants should be supported in the development of their personal and professional skills

AIM
To consider what makes staff development (INSET) effective, and to examine the possible benefits of assistants and teachers learning together.

LEFT UP IN THE AIR

Cameo: An assistant speculates about staff development she feels is needed:

> If we had a workshop, all together, led by the science coordinator, it would help with the whole business of making sure we're doing the right thing as far as the curriculum is concerned. Neither of us was particularly good at school, it would help us to do some practical activities as a group.

STAFF DEVELOPMENT (INSET) EVALUATION EXERCISE

Individually:
Each fill in the sheets provided, answering the questions on each one.

Use the cameo above to stimulate your thoughts on the matter.

Do this without chatting to others.

As a group:
1. Split into four working groups (pairs or more).
2. Each group takes a set of sheets (A,B,C or D).
3. Analyse what is written on your set of sheets and list what are the main points offered by all the participants' ideas.
4. Record these on a single flipchart sheet and choose a spokesperson.
5. Feed back to the whole group your main points.

Now draw up your action plan.

Some questions to guide your discussion:
- What are the implications for the school staff development plan about which forms of staff development (INSET) this staff group feels are effective?
- How will the assistants' needs be better met?
- How will the teams' needs be better met?
- Are there any ideas which members of the school staff can plan and organise for colleagues?
- What skills are available to assist this? What resources?
- From who else, and where else, will support be needed?

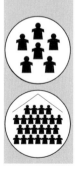

Help in the Classroom

STAFF DEVELOPMENT (INSET) EVALUATION

A. Identify a recent INSET development that you have been involved in either as provider or receiver. It can be in or out of school, one day or a series of sessions, etc.

What were the actual outcomes for pupils?

- ✂ - - - -

B. Identify the strengths of the activity.

C. Identify the weaknesses of the activity.

✂ -

D. Identify the links between the activity and benefits for you and your work in the classroom.

Assistant   Teacher

Identify the links between the activity and benefits for the pupils.

STAFF DEVELOPMENT NEEDS

AIM

To consider the ways in which adults, both teachers and assistants, learn best and how staff development planning should take account of this. An activity known as 'critical incident analysis' is used to bring into focus positive learning experiences and the factors which bring these about. This is based on the work of Tripp (1994) and Woods (1994). The interaction between individual learning styles and forms of learning opportunity offered for staff in primary schools is considered, through an initial analysis of personal critical incidents in learning.

Individually:

Think of a moment that you feel made a significant impact on your learning which happened in the last term or so, using the analysis sheet to help you.

- What was so significant about it?
- How and when did it happen?
- What impact did it have on your practice, i.e. what difference did it make to the way you understand, plan, manage and carry out your practice?

In pairs:

Compare what you have each written.

Think about the situations in which you each experienced this incident.

- How similar or different were they?
- Was this due to your preferred way of learning, e.g. a lecture, working in activity groups, or working with the children?
- Was it due to the situation, environment, person from whom you were learning, or topic?

Small groups:

1. Record on a flipchart what each of your incidents was.
2. Write down the way in which each of the learning situations had been planned and by whom.
3. Mark any that you had direct involvement in planning yourself.
4. Keep the flipchart until the next meeting of this group.

Individually:

Reflect on what you have learnt about your own learning.

Finish the Reflection sentences on the analysis sheet.

Staff Development Needs   111

STAFF DEVELOPMENT NEEDS

AIM

To consider the impact of individual critical incidents on learning and their links to planning staff development opportunities for teachers and assistants in the school. This is done through the completion of a timeline, based on the ideas of Ainscow *et al.* (1994a), which has staff development opportunities offered to individuals in the last term (or two) listed on it, along with the flexibility for individuals to add their own ideas. The activity also builds on the previous one, moving from a pairs and small group activity to a larger group, possibly all the staff in the school, evaluating the impact of their learning and the contexts in which the individuals' significant incidents occurred.

Individually:

1. Consider the outline you have. The coordinator has put in some key events on the timeline to start you off.
2. If you weren't there or can't remember any of them make a note. (This in itself tells you something important!)
3. Complete the timeline putting in any additional learning experiences which were important to you and made a significant impact on your learning and practice.

In pairs:

Compare what you have put on your timelines.

Were any events already on there significant to your learning?

What have you each added?

In small groups:

1. Consider what you have on your timelines and if you have it, the flipchart you put together at the last session. In evaluating your learning in the context of what the school planned for you:
   - What were the most positive experiences?
   - What were their features?
   - Did you help to plan them?
   - Were they part of an individual needs analysis which informed the staff development plan?
2. Draw up a list of advice about how to bring about critical incidents in learning for this particular group (no more than six pertinent and priority features).
3. Put these on a flipchart, add diagrams or drawings to make an impact and post this up on the wall.

Whole group:

Form new groups by dividing participants into the same number of groups as you have posters, with a representative of each poster in the new groups.

Conduct a 'poster tour' which gives everyone an opportunity to see all the posters while hearing from one of its authors why this was written in the way it was.

Discuss as a whole group what you have learnt from this activity and which points should be added into staff development planning as a result.

Individually:

From your own perspective, for example as assistant, teacher, manager, staff development coordinator, or learning support coordinator, write a personal action point about what has been discussed and what you might do as a result.

STAFF DEVELOPMENT NEEDS

CRITICAL INCIDENT ANALYSIS

Think of a moment that you feel made a significant impact on your learning in the last term or so in such a way that it has changed the way you work.

Notes:

Consider how much this was due to your preferred way of learning, e.g. from a book, a lecture, working in activity groups, or working on programmes for the children/students.

Notes:

Think about whether it was due to factors such as the situation, environment, person from whom you were learning, or topic.

Notes:

Reflection:

I learn best when . . .

I learn in a context which . . .

I learn from . . .

STAFF DEVELOPMENT NEEDS

CRITICAL INCIDENTS IN LEARNING TIMELINE

Term: *Date:*

Staff development day(s)

Staff development session/meeting/workshop(s)

Departmental/year group meeting(s)

Classroom partnership work

Something outside school

Additional critical incidents of learning

Term: *Date:*

STAFF DEVELOPMENT NEEDS

AIM
To consider the ways in which adults, both teachers and assistants, learn best and how staff development planning should take account of this. An activity known as 'critical incident analysis' is used to bring into focus positive learning experiences and the factors which bring these about. This is based on the work of Tripp (1994) and Woods (1994). The interaction between individual learning styles and forms of learning opportunity offered for staff in secondary schools is considered, through an initial analysis of personal critical incidents in learning.

Individually:
Think of a moment that you feel made a significant impact on your learning which happened in the last term or so, using the analysis sheet to help you.

- What was so significant about it?
- How and when did it happen?
- What impact did it have on your practice, i.e. what difference did it make to the way you understand, plan, manage and carry out your practice?

In pairs:
Compare what you have each written.

Think about the situations in which you each experienced this incident.

- How similar or different were they?
- Was this due to your preferred way of learning, e.g. a lecture, working in activity groups, liaising with a curriculum department, or working with the students?
- Was it due to the situation, environment, person from whom you were learning, or topic?

Small groups:
1. Record on a flipchart what each of your incidents was.
2. Write down the way in which each of the learning situations had been planned and by whom.
3. Mark any that you had direct involvement in planning yourself.
4. Keep the flipchart until the next meeting of this group.

Individually:
Reflect on what you have learnt about your own learning.

Finish the Reflection sentences on the analysis sheet.

STAFF DEVELOPMENT NEEDS

AIM

To consider the impact of individual critical incidents on learning and their links to planning staff development opportunities for teachers and assistants in the school. This is done through the completion of a timeline, based on the ideas of Ainscow *et al.* (1994a), which has staff development opportunities offered to individuals in the last term (or two) listed on it, along with the flexibility for individuals to add their own ideas. The activity also builds on the previous one, moving from a pairs and small group activity to a larger group, possibly all the staff in the school, evaluating the impact of their learning and the contexts in which the individuals' significant incidents occurred.

Individually:

1. Consider the outline you have. The coordinator has put in some key events on the timeline to start you off.

2. If you weren't there or can't remember any of them make a note. (This in itself tells you something important!)

3. Complete the timeline putting in any additional learning experiences which were important to you and made a significant impact on your learning and practice.

In pairs:

Compare what you have put on your timelines.

Were any events already on there significant to your learning?

What have you each added?

In small groups:

1. Consider what you have on your timelines and if you have it, the flipchart you put together at the last session. In evaluating your learning in the context of what the school planned for you.

   • What were the most positive experiences?

   • What were their features?

   • Did you help to plan them?

   • Were they part of an individual needs analysis which informed the staff development plan?

2. Draw up a list of advice about how to bring about critical incidents in learning for this particular group (no more than six pertinent and priority features)

3. Put these on a flipchart, add diagrams or drawings to make an impact and post this up on the wall.

Whole group:

   • Form new groups by dividing participants into the same number of groups as you have posters, with a representative of each poster in the new groups.

   • Conduct a 'poster tour' which gives everyone an opportunity to see all the posters while hearing from one of its authors why this was written in the way it was.

   • Discuss as a whole group what you have learnt from this activity and which points should be added into staff development planning as a result.

Individually:

From your own perspective, for example as assistant, teacher, manager, curriculum department leader, staff development coordinator, or learning support coordinator, write a personal action point about what has been discussed and what you might do as a result.

STAFF DEVELOPMENT NEEDS

AIM

To develop further the review of assistants' learning, in particular with and alongside other members of staff. Action plans that have been in operation are considered, progress is reviewed and further needs, sources of support and staff development are considered and action plans updated as a result. A continuing emphasis is placed on developing existing confidence, competencies and skills, and the role of other members of staff in supporting this process. Planning a visit to a part of this school not normally seen/visited/worked in, or a visit to another school to observe interesting practice and meet other practitioners, is a strategy suggested.

Individually:

Reflect on your progress with your focus for development.

Use the review sheet to do this, writing some notes for yourself.

In pairs:

Tell each other how you have been getting on; what has been positive; what you have learnt; whether it has made a difference to your practice in classrooms.

Explore difficulties you have had, how you have overcome them and whether you have had sufficient support.

Individually:

Think of your focus for development. Is there somewhere in this school (or another one) where there is some practice that you think would be interesting or relevant to your focus?

Use the school visit plan to help you to think of what you might do.

In pairs:

Talk to each other about your ideas for a visit.

Would it be helpful to go with a partner, if this is possible, so that you can discuss what you have seen? If so, who would be best?

Help one another to draw up a feasible plan which has a realistic timescale, and suggestions about whose support you may need to do it, for example the learning support coordinator or the person who deals with timetabling.

Whole group:
- Each person tells the whole group what *their partner* intends to do.
- The coordinator of the discussion makes a note of resources or sources of support that the assistants will need.
- The coordinator may need to assist with strategies for finding out and collecting information.
- Agree a date/meeting when the pairs and this group can review progress.

ONGOING PROGRESS REPORT ON STAFF DEVELOPMENT NEEDS

Date:

How I feel it is going:

What I have learnt:

How and where I have learnt it, e.g. alongside teachers in class/staff development sessions, out of school on a course:

How I have been supported by (give names of identified sources of support):

Problems I have had:

Further needs/issues I need support with:

Next steps:

SCHOOL VISIT PLAN AND REPORT

Date: *Date of visit:*   *Place:*

Why I have chosen this part of our school/another school:

Who I might do the visit with:

What I am going to look for/observe and how I will do it (NB a clear focus and strategy is essential):

What I found out:

References

Ainscow, M., Hargreaves, D. H., Hopkins, D., Balshaw, M. H., Black-Hawkins, K. (1994a) *Mapping Change in Schools*. Cambridge: University of Cambridge.

Ainscow, M., Hopkins, D., Southworth, G., West, M. (1994b) *Creating the Conditions for School Improvement*. London: David Fulton Publishers.

Ainscow, M. (1998) *Reaching out to all learners: some lessons from experience*. Address given at the International Conference on School Effectiveness and Improvement. Manchester, January 1998.

Balshaw, M. H. (1991) *Help in the Classroom, 1st edn*. London: David Fulton Publishers.

Balshaw, M. H. (1996a) *Partnership dialogue: learning through research together*. Unpublished discussion paper.

Balshaw, M. H. (1996b) *Redefining consultation through collaborative inquiry: some experiences and challenges*. Unpublished paper presented at the American Educational Research Association Annual Meeting, New York, April 1996.

Balshaw, M. H. (1998) *Inquiry-based consultancy: towards school development*. Unpublished doctoral thesis presented to the University of Cambridge, 1998.

Balshaw, M. H., Crebbin, B., Fowler, M., Lucas, H., Moore, J., Perry, J., Smith, G., Winter, M. (1997) *Insiders' voices: personal and public theorising about professional learning and practice in schools* Unpublished paper presented at the American Educational Research Association Annual Meeting, Chicago, March 1997.

Department for Education and Employment (1997) *Excellence for All*, Green Paper. London: HMSO.

Department of Education and Science (1978) *Special Educational Needs, The Warnock Report*. London: HMSO.

Fox, G. (1993) *A Handbook for Special Needs Assistants*. London: David Fulton Publishers.

Fox, G. (1998) *A Handbook for Learning Support Assistants*. London: David Fulton Publishers.

Fullan, M. (1990) 'Staff development, innovation, and institutional development', in Joyce, B. (ed.) *Changing School Culture Through Staff Development*. New York: ASCD.

Fullan, M. (1991) *The New Meaning of Educational Change*. New York: Teachers College Press.

Fullan, M. (1993) *Change Forces: Probing the Depths of Educational Reform*. London: Cassell.

Fullan, M. (1995) 'The school as a learning organisation: distant dreams', *Theory into Practice*, **34**(4) 230–235.

Fullan, M. and Hargreaves, A. (1992) *What's Worth Fighting for in Your School?* Milton Keynes: Open University Press.

Fullan, M. and Park, P. (1981) *Curriculum Implementation*. Toronto: Ministry of Education.

Hargreaves, A. (1998) *The emotions in the politics of educational change*. Unpublished paper presented at the International Congress of School Effectiveness and Improvement, Manchester, January 1998.

Johnson, D. W. and Johnson, R. T. (1989) *Leading the Co-operative School*. Edina: Interaction Book Company.

Lorenz, S. (1998) *Effective In-class Support*. London: David Fulton Publishers.

Reason, P. (1988) *Human Inquiry in Action*. London: Sage Publications.

Sebba, J. and Sachdev, D. (1997) *What Works in Inclusive Education?* London: Barnardos.

Senge, P. (1990) *The Fifth Discipline*. London: Century Business Books.

Thousand, J. S. and Villa, R. (1991) 'Accommodation for greater student variance', in Ainscow, M. *Effective Schools for All*. London: David Fulton Publishers.

Tripp, D. (1994) 'Teachers' lives, critical incidents, and professional practice', *International Journal of Qualitative Studies in Education* 7(1), 65–76.

Unesco (1990) *World Declaration on Education for All and Framework for Action to Meet Basic Learning Needs*. Thailand: Jomtien.

Unesco (1991) *Special Needs in the Classroom: a teacher education resource pack*. Paris: Unesco.

Unesco (1994) *The Salamanca Statement and Framework for Action*. Paris: Unesco; Madrid: Ministry of Education and Science.

West, M. and Ainscow, M. (1991) *Managing School Development*. London: David Fulton Publishers.

Woods, P. (1994) 'Collaborating in historical ethnography: researching critical events in education', *International Journal of Qualitative Studies in Education* 7(4), 309–321.